Beginning Shakespeare 4–11

D0497360

'This book is clear, approachable, and true. The elegant simplicity of its good guidance is the product of years of practical experience in the classroom. I wholeheartedly commend it to primary school teachers everywhere.'

Michael Boyd, Artistic Director of the Royal Shakespeare Company

Shakespeare's plays are widely regarded as the greatest inheritance in English literature and recent years have seen a growing interest in introducing them to children in their primary schools. In this book, the authors bring a blend of clear thinking, playful and inventive practice and straightforward practical advice to bear on teaching Shakespeare in the primary school.

Children who encounter Shakespeare early have the opportunity to become comfortable with the plays, their stories, characters and settings, long before they might become intimidated by their associations with exclusivity and 'high' culture. They are also given the chance to become familiar with and absorb his powerful and complex language at a stage when they are constantly encountering new vocabulary. To do this most effectively demands a dynamic pedagogy, one which recognises that the plays are best explored and understood through active, physical engagement.

Beginning Shakespeare 4–11 offers a sound rationale for teaching Shakespeare in primary schools and shows how to engage children with Shakespeare through story, through the very best of early years practice, and through his rich and sensual language. It also illustrates how engagement with the plays and their language can have a dramatic impact on children's writing. And because plays are for performing, there is helpful and practical advice on how to develop the work and share it with the whole school, parents and the wider community.

This accessible and comprehensive guide is ideal for teacher trainees and practising primary teachers everywhere.

Joe Winston is Professor of Drama and Arts Education at the University of Warwick and has served as co-editor of *Research in Drama Education* since 2005.

Miles Tandy is Head of Education Partnerships at the Royal Shakespeare Company. He has worked previously as a teacher, school leader and local authority adviser.

Beginning Shakespeare 4–11

Joe Winston and Miles Tandy

Routledge
Taylor & Francis Group

LONDON AND NEW YORK

First published 2012
by Routledge
2 Park Square, Milton Park, Abingdon, Oxon OX14 4RN

Simultaneously published in the USA and Canada
by Routledge
711 Third Avenue, New York, NY 10017

Routledge is an imprint of the Taylor & Francis Group, an informa business

British Library Cataloguing in Publication Data
A catalogue record for this book is available from the British Library

Library of Congress Cataloging in Publication Data
Winston, Joe, 1953–
Beginning Shakespeare 4–11 / Joe Winston and Miles Tandy.
p. cm.
Includes bibliographical references.
1. Shakespeare, William, 1564–1616—Study and teaching. I. Tandy, Miles. II.
Title. III. Title: Beginning Shakespeare four to eleven.
PR2987.W56 2012
822.3'3—dc23
2012003470

ISBN 978-0-415-61846-5 (hbk)
ISBN 978-0-415-61848-9 (pbk)
ISBN 978-0-203-11770-5 (ebk)

Typeset in Galliard
by Book Now Ltd, London

MIX
Paper from
responsible sources
FSC
www.fsc.org   FSC® C004839

Printed and bound in Great Britain by
TJ International Ltd, Padstow, Cornwall

Dedicated to the memory of Francisca Tandy (1955–2009) who once played Cobweb when she was seven, and to Máire Tandy (1916–2001) who made the costume.

Contents

Foreword

Like skiing, it's never too early to start on Shakespeare. That's the good news. But even as this book is written, each generation's relationship to Shakespeare's language is slipping like melting ice caps into an icy past. Perhaps this book can be the beginning of reversing that trend!

The first steps in Shakespeare will plant the knowledge of character and plot and all those empowering offshoots that will enable the young viewer to go to the theatre and 'catch on' quickly. But, more excitingly, Shakespeare's words are so planted in the language muscle that they will allow the young student to learn his games with language even as they learn language itself. Shakespeare was inventing the architecture of the English we speak today, at the time of writing, adding new words to the language, playing with and using the iambic pentameter like a lasso and sometimes abandoning it to greater effect; reversing it or sharing it with another speaker. His great achievements were to unite thought with feeling so that they became the same thing, and to make rhythm the key to the unconscious, by which I mean making the truth of the person emerge in how they speak, not just what they say. The misrepresentation of Shakespeare's language is that it is complicated at the cliff face of the 'word', but that is not really true.

Some of the best lines in Shakespeare are the simplest. 'I have done the deed,' says Macbeth after the murder of Duncan. At his most powerful, Shakespeare plunges back into our atavistic selves to find the right words, which are often ancient and monosyllabic. 'When shall we three meet again?' ask the witches at the start of Macbeth and unknown to young and old reader the very iambic, which marks the rhythm of so much of his work is, through the magical spell, reversed. Instead of *tee tum tee tum tee tum tee tum tee tum* we are receiving the more disquieting *tum tee tum tee tum tee tum tee tum tee*. Not that one should ever need to speak on these stresses; they exist under the language like a drum beat that reminds us to keep going forward and not look back!

So we shall find that rhythm, which children are so disposed to in their play, as the way into the plays and it always holds the emotional state of the character and reveals their inner selves. When Katherine, in *The Taming of the Shrew*, says:

But if it were, doubt not her care should be
To comb your noddle with a three-legged stool
And paint your face and use you like a fool

It is childish as it is childlike – rhyme and a fury to match. At the end of that play Katherine changes and speaks with more eloquence than anyone else in her world, sculpting phrases that, with the Mona Lisa smile, have the world in awe at her enigma: 'Thy husband is thy lord, thy life, thy keeper, thy head, thy sovereign.' Do we detect a forced calm? Try it aloud and see!

And what about dramatic reversals in simple lines packed with contradiction? The Princess of France, on discovering that her father has died, says in a quip that stops the play in its tracks: 'Dead, for my life!'. And there begins her growing up. Nothing difficult to remember – just short words meeting at a moment of catastrophe. If one attends to them they grow in stature before one's eyes. In the philosophic realm we have the famous 'To be, or not to be, that is the question': a phrase that has in it the beginning of what will serve the reader well later; the dialectic that marks so much of Shakespeare's neo-Platonism. Served in this iconic phrase, one half of the sentence is met in the second half: the beginning of philosophical discussion declared like a headline in a line. The thought then develops and the student actor can follow as much as her or his abilities allow.

What is helpful is that Shakespeare always gives the premise of the argument at the beginning, so one is always 'on track'. All later writing deals with shades of deceit or self-deception, but not this writer.

He also manages to give direction to the audience. Here is the most playful stage direction of all time, as much fun for the four-year-old as for the adult. All can enjoy the game. Oberon in *A Midsummer Night's Dream* leans forward to the audience and declares 'I am invisible!'. At that moment we all collude, nod and agree as our imaginations make it happen. We see him and make the impossible occur – no one else in his world, the stage, can. This mutually mad magic rivals any Harry Potter cloak as it proceeds to hold our attention, to make it so.

All of this delight awaits the young discoverer and the teacher. Shakespeare maps the internal world by taking human speech, turning it into poetry and returning it into the mouth of the characters as if it were human speech. Despite holding the whole play in rhythm, characters find their own individual shapes. So Celia in *As You Like It* is quite different from Rosalind: one talks in short bursts; the other in sweeping sentences: 'No, No, Orlando, men are April when they woo, December when they wed. Maids are May when they are maids, but the sky changes when they are wives.' So no two characters speak alike. His is a pure genius that allows for audiences to judge subtly what they hear. We are therefore part of an extravagant enhancement but we need only enjoy it to experience it. He is daring to name the human condition that was so hard to extrapolate in the hundreds of years before, by the use of often-simple devices. He uses external images to tell us of internal feelings. We speak the thought but it evokes emotion.

It is as if Shakespeare has written nearly all the notation necessary and gives an invitation to the reader or actor to make the words live and always live for that particular line and that reader. So Shakespeare is for all men, all women and all children: a great individualist who hides nothing and yet only we, in each level of understanding, reveal it. He makes artists of us all because he dances with the child in himself.

Fiona Shaw
London 2012

Acknowledgements

The practice which is at the heart of this book had its genesis in an extraordinary community of practitioners. We would particularly like to thank everyone in the Education Department of the Royal Shakespeare Company, especially Rachel Gartside, Mary Johnson, Jamie Luck, Jacqui O'Hanlon and Helen Phipps. Our thanks also extend to Astrid Cheng, Jo Howell, Andy Kempe and Jonothan Neelands; and to all the teachers and children who have collaborated with us to put this work into practice, in particular everyone at Dashwood Primary School in Banbury. Finally, our love and gratitude go to the ever-patient Gill and Denise.

Introduction

Here's an idea. Let's get rid of Shakespeare, or at least quietly forget about him. All that archaic language and overacting, those interminable soliloquies and dreadful puns that pretentious people like to claim they appreciate. There are plenty of good modern plays, modern poems, modern stories, far more relevant to contemporary concerns, aren't there? Anyway, why should someone who has been dead for nearly 400 years exercise such a stranglehold over our culture? And – be honest – how many of us nowadays bother going to see his plays, anyway? Or, if we do, how many of us deep down find him, well, boring? And if we are talking about children in primary schools doing Shakespeare, isn't this rather misguided? If most adults find him difficult, irrelevant and boring, surely this will be exacerbated in the case of children. Surely primary schools these days face challenges enough trying to teach children – more and more of whom do not speak English as a first language – to speak, read and write straightforward, simple English, the kind they are going to need to pass exams and get a job. So what is the point of Shakespeare?

Since you have gone so far as to pick up or purchase this book, you yourself probably do not think this way but perhaps you can think of friends and colleagues who would feel some sympathy with the argument posed above. Shakespeare can, indeed, seem remote, difficult and irrelevant to many people who are far from unintelligent but who find their cultural enjoyment elsewhere; and for whom social class is arguably the key determinant as to whether or not they like Shakespeare. As one young boy from inner-city Coventry recently told a colleague of ours: 'Shakespeare is for posh people, not for us'.

Of course, we don't agree with him or with any of the points made in the opening paragraph. On the contrary, we believe that Shakespeare is for everyone, including children from deprived backgrounds and those with English as an additional language (EAL); that his stories and verse can make a rich and vital contribution to their language development, their creative thinking and their moral imaginations; and that all of this is achievable in ways that support rather than distract from their overall educational attainment, including their test scores. This book is intended to provide you with practical ways to teach Shakespeare in your classroom, as part of your curriculum, in ways that will be both rewarding to yourself and accessible, enjoyable and motivating to the children you teach. By way of addressing any lingering scepticism, however, we begin with a rationale as to why Shakespeare can be appealing and fascinating to children in primary schools and why we believe his work can be of broad educational benefit to them.

Shakespeare is not boring

Ask any class of children if they like stories and, whether they are avid readers or not even able to read yet, very few – if any – will tell you that they do not. Then ask them what kind of stories they like and you can probably predict the sort of responses you will receive: funny stories and scary stories; stories with ghosts and larger-than-life evil characters who nevertheless get defeated in the end; love stories and fairy stories and the kind of stories in which there is magic and magical creatures who play all kinds of tricks on people; tales of conflict and war between rival kings and queens. Older children in primary schools may well tell you they prefer horror stories, with murder and plenty of blood. Shakespeare has all of these ingredients and plenty more – the common currency of popular stories throughout history and across cultures. What is more, they are never simple in terms of their plotting or their moral thrust. There are as many complications, reversals, deceptions and misunderstandings in plays like *Twelfth Night*, *Richard III* and *Macbeth* as you will find in a shelf full of the best-loved children's novels.

If Shakespeare's stories are not boring, then perhaps the problem lies in the language. There is no denying that his language can be a barrier to understanding for adults as well as children but this is principally due to the way it is approached. Often this is with a pious sense of reverence. Rather like Latin in the old Roman Catholic mass, the language is sometimes treated as sacred text, not so much to be understood as to be endured in the belief that listening to the words can spiritually nourish one's soul. Bad productions of his tragedies, for example, professional as well as amateur, often feature actors declaiming the lines with a theatrical gravitas that does little to convey their subtleties of meaning to their respectfully silent audiences. In UK secondary schools, where the study of Shakespeare's text has, until recently, been a compulsory part of national examinations at the age of 14, the problem has been rather the opposite; key passages are over-analysed for meaning at the expense of experiencing and enjoying the sensual qualities of their sounds and rhythms; something we will return to later.

As a primary teacher, you need neither be unnecessarily intimidated by Shakespeare's language nor overly earnest about it. You should see it as open to selective editing and adaptation, always the servant of the story, with children's enjoyment a priority. Most importantly, you should have your children use the language as it was meant to be used, namely, as words to be spoken, whose possible meanings are best explored through active, physical means, through the power and subtleties of the voice working together with the gestures and actions of the body. Then – and only then – will Shakespeare come to life in your classroom.

Shakespeare is playful

One thing the vast majority of children love to do is play. Whether it is games, sports, fantasy play, dressing up, teasing, joking, pretence of all kinds, children do not see play as a chore but as a release, as liberating and exhilarating. That is why Michael Boyd, the current artistic director of the Royal Shakespeare Company, has described children as 'geniuses at playing'.[1] But we are wrong to think that play is something that only children do – adults play, too, all of the time, and are deeply interested in its many forms. We play sports, music, video games and various games of skill and chance, such as cards; every time we watch a film, a TV series or a piece of theatre, we know we are watching people play. In our own lives we might engage in many forms of playful language – punning, joking, exaggerating, using simile and metaphor, making witty or ironic comments – particularly with those with whom we are intimate or friendly. On the other hand, we may use such play in more aggressive forms when we are angry or hurt, as sarcasm or as the kind of banter which has an edge of menace or insult to it. We often enjoy discussing various kinds of play we have observed, such as a football match, a rock concert or a movie. If we sing along to a song on the radio, we are often drawn to it by its playful use of rhythm, rhyme, stress and intonation, as much as by its melody. At other times we may well feel that much of our lives is spent playing a specific role. If you are a primary teacher, you will undoubtedly have your way of looking and sounding cross in order to obtain silence; of appearing to be delighted at a piece of work or particular answer; of looking puzzled or mystified as you pretend to be baffled by a particular mathematical problem. Learning how to play the role of teacher successfully is part and parcel of becoming an effective one.

Shakespeare knew this, of course. 'All the world's a stage,' he famously wrote, 'And all the men and women merely players'. He knew that we play different social roles throughout our lives and that we are fascinated by watching people perform these roles – the lover, the leader, the son/daughter, the colleague/friend – and the various ways they can be played out for better or for worse. He shows us the romantic lover (Romeo) and the hapless lover (Malvolio, in *Twelfth Night*); the heroic leader (Henry V) and the weak leader (Richard II); the dutiful daughter (Cordelia) and the rebellious daughter (Kate, in *Taming of the Shrew*); the devoted friend (Kent in *King Lear*) and the treacherous friend (Iago in *Othello*). All of these characters consciously play a role and do so by using language in the ways we have listed above, through imagery, irony and all manner of word play to cajole, impress, console, persuade, deceive or insult. Shakespeare is so good at this that his characters have become iconic; Romeo as the man who knows how to use words to woo a woman; Henry as the leader who knows how to rouse his troops to victory; Iago as the false friend who uses words to poison a good man's heart. These are serious players indeed! And integral to how they use language to such great effect is the way they manipulate its formal qualities; rhythm, rhyme, imagery and sonority matter as much to them as do the literal meanings of their words.

Very young children are drawn to language through such formal qualities as these. Nursery rhymes hold their attention through strongly accentuated rhythms and intonations and children are often happy to hear and speak them again and again. As they grow, their liking for the playful qualities of language persists in skipping rhymes, playground chants, jokes, nonsense verse and in the lyrics of pop songs and hip-hop. The ready appeal of such word play is there to be harnessed in order to draw children into the world that Shakespeare so vividly evokes through his language. All we, as teachers, need are the pedagogic resources to do so. And these should make use of children's love of play by being playful themselves, in all kind of ways, to mirror and echo Shakespeare's own playfulness. As we do this, we will know that, although children will outgrow the world of nursery and skipping rhymes, no one ever outgrows Shakespeare; once hooked, he can be with them as a resource to nourish them culturally for the rest of their lives.

As teachers, we need to recognise that children know all about and are drawn to the more aggressive forms of language play, too; those found in taunts, insults, back-answering and chants between rival groups, all of which are abundantly present in Shakespeare. You might understandably flinch at the idea of such darker forms of language play being encouraged in your own classroom. But, in Shakespeare's work, the colourful and tense language of insult and aggression is not directed at anyone in the classroom but at people in a fiction. Children can enjoy the cursing of Caliban in *The Tempest* and the way Achilles and Hector square up to each other in *Troilus and Cressida* as resonant of real life but as safely ring-fenced from it. Within the protective fence of fiction, language can channel and defuse rather than provoke aggression. As Shakespeare's contemporary, Thomas Kidd, expressed it: 'Where words prevaile not, violence prevailes'.[2]

Shakespeare is useful

Shakespeare's plays may well be set in times and places remote from children's experience, yet they deal with the moral realities of life, many of which children will know about at first hand. To draw from the examples above: most children will have plenty of ideas about the kind of things good daughters and bad daughters might do or say to their parents; they will know how it feels to be badly let down or betrayed by a friend; and they will be able to talk about those adults or friends who know how to exercise authority well and those who don't.

So, Shakespeare's plays are not just good, entertaining stories told in beautiful language; like the best kind of stories, they make us think about important issues that never go away because they are about what makes us human. Often the characters find themselves in situations where they need to make choices that are difficult, such as Hamlet; or where they must face the consequences of their choices, such as Brutus or Macbeth. Should Juliet choose love for her family over love for Romeo, whose family is at war with hers? In Shylock's case, what constitutes the boundary between justice and vengeance and does he deserve what happens to him? Even Shakespeare's comedies present us with questions which are strikingly problematic. We might well feel that someone like Malvolio in *Twelfth Night* deserves to be made a fool of, but when does a practical joke go too far? When does it turn into bullying? Shakespeare's dramatic situations and dilemmas are doubtless more extreme than those that most children will have to face but they nonetheless resonate with what they know and understand about the world and their own place in it.

When children are helped to connect morally and emotionally with these stories they can be taken on a journey that challenges them to extend the range of their moral imaginations. In this way, we can regard Shakespeare's work as foundational in two, inter-related senses of the word. They are foundational texts within our own culture, part of a shared repertoire of stories capable of informing public discourse on a range of political and moral issues; they are also foundational at the personal level of individual children, a secular resource to help them wonder about the larger political and social world to which we all belong.

Shakespeare is powerful

Shakespeare is powerful, then, in a number of ways; his language can evoke and arouse powerful emotions; his stories can exercise a powerful grip on our imaginations; and his themes deal with all kinds of human problems that are still powerfully relevant to us today.

Yet Shakespeare is powerful in another, very straightforward way; he is generally judged by people whose opinions matter to be one of the most supreme artists ever to have lived. You can argue with this judgement of course, and certain people do – some cleverly, others not so cleverly – but, whatever you or I might think, this does not detract from the fact that to know about Shakespeare, to be able to discuss, appreciate and quote from his plays is seen as one of the key markers of a good education by influential people, be they politicians, cultural commentators or business leaders. Knowing about Shakespeare, and feeling that Shakespeare speaks to you as much as to anyone else, can help you to feel part of the culture of the powerful. In other words, it can influence what powerful people think about you and whether they will be prepared to listen to you or not. Shakespeare, in other words, can be one of the ways in which a child's education can help to provide them with a voice.

People know this implicitly. Often those whose social class and/or social marginalisation has led them to dismiss Shakespeare aggressively nonetheless feel resentment at being excluded from this 'club'. Conversely, there are those from more privileged social backgrounds who were taught Shakespeare badly, have never liked him, yet would be loath to admit this for fear of appearing uncultured and ignorant. Such feelings of inadequacy can damage self-esteem and limit aspirations, whereas a good education in Shakespeare can have the opposite effect. If being spoken *down* to can damage a person's feeling of self-worth, we may venture that no one was ever hurt by being spoken *up* to.

Remember, and tell your children this: Shakespeare himself was a commoner, the son of a glover, educated in a local school, who never had the chance to go to university. He grew up among ordinary people and, although his plays were performed in front of royalty and the aristocracy, he had a massive public following. Less than ten per cent of the audience who came to watch them in the Globe Theatre could read. They didn't feel excluded or patronised but found in his stories and language a vibrant, cultural resource. Shakespeare for them was the best, and he still is; and he can be for our children today.

Chapter 1

Beginning Shakespeare with games

In the Introduction, we have argued that the spirit of play and playfulness is central to Shakespeare's work and that this needs to be reflected in the pedagogic approaches we adopt. In this way we will tap not only into children's liking for play but also into the ludic energy at the heart of the plays themselves. Games are a straightforward way for us to do this and there are some key comparisons to bear in mind when considering their place in our teaching of Shakespeare.

Games are like stories

Shakespeare was a storyteller who knew how to work with a variety of popular story forms, including fairy tales, romances, tales of heroes, tales of the supernatural and tales of revenge. Such stories are generally organised around typical characters and plot patterns that unfold in ways that are in many ways predictable but also capable of infinite variation. It is how authors manage this tension between predictability and variation that largely determines how successful they are. Of course, the complexity of theme and characterisation are far greater in Shakespeare's plays, but the raw elements are still there for young children to recognise and respond to. A child who loves fairy tales will know that, in *The Winter's Tale*, the beautiful young country girl, who is really a princess, and with whom the prince falls in love, will, in the end, marry him and be happily re-united with her family; she just won't be sure *how* this ending will come about. On the other hand, a child who likes tales of the supernatural will suspect that Macbeth cannot play with the devil and win but will be intrigued to know just *how* he will lose.

Games, too, progress through patterns and stages that work around predictability and variation, setting up a series of expectations and surprises. So, in every game of 'Wink murder', children will know that someone is the murderer but they won't know who; they will hope to discover the murderer's identity but know that they may well be killed before doing so; and they will know that, by the time the game ends, a number of people will have died but they won't know how many. As there is, then, an underlying link between *games competence* and *literary competence*,[1] the narrative pattern of a game can sometimes be adapted to suggest or mirror or resonate with the patterns of a particular story. This connection can be deepened if the game itself is presented within the fictional frame of the story in question.

Games are organised like heated dialogues

There are lots of arguments, heated discussions and debates in Shakespeare's plays. Often these take the form of quick-fire verbal exchanges, such as we find famously in Act I, Scene 1 of *Romeo and Juliet* ('Do you bite your thumb at us sir? / I do bite my thumb, sir!') and in the following exchange between Hamlet and his mother in Act II, Scene 4:

Queen: Hamlet, thou hast thy father much offended.
Hamlet: Mother, you have my father much offended.
Queen: Come, come, you answer with an idle tongue.
Hamlet: Go, go, you question with a wicked tongue.

Exchanges such as these gain their energy from the rhythm and pattern of the turn taking, in which the characters attempt to match and outdo one another.

Competitive games, whether language-based or not, tend to work through a similarly equitable distribution of turn taking. This is true of chess, for example, of numerous card games, of ball games such as tennis, and even of such placid word-based games as 'I spy' and 'Twenty questions'. Such games resonate with the qualities of a dialogue or an argument because each participant has their turn to speak or act but must attend and/or listen to the contributions of others if they are to perform well.

Games have an in-built, ambivalent moral energy

Shakespeare's plays release us from the everyday; for a few hours we are willingly taken far away from our daily lives and can imagine thinking and behaving very differently from our everyday patterns. As we argued in the Introduction, his plays deal with moral issues without being moralistic. In other words, they don't impose answers on us. They don't tell us how we should behave when we leave the theatre – a theatre is not a church, after all – but deal at a deep level with issues that are central to our humanity. It is the very act of feeling and thinking about these issues that can broaden children's moral horizons.

Games do something similar. For a short period of time, when we play a game, we behave differently than in our normal everyday lives because the rules are clearly different. Children have to obey many rules in schools, rules that are explicit, enforceable, not much fun and often begin with the word 'Don't ...' – 'Don't run down the corridor', for example, or 'Don't shout out an answer in class'. Such rules are imposed on them. Games, on the other hand, work through rules that most children appreciate and willingly opt into as they understand implicitly that sticking to them is what makes the game enjoyable. The rules of a game will help children know when it is their turn, how to play the game properly and success-fully, who, if anyone, is on their side, and what happens if they transgress the rules in any way. But one of the key functions of such rules is to make the game fair. Without being didactic, then, games can teach children about fairness by working with their implicit sense of justice, so helping to exemplify and develop it.

Games provide a space for children not only to co-operate and work in teams but also to display individual skills and such challenges will readily find a place within the personal and social education policy of a primary school. But the more competitive games provide space within their rules for children to learn about guile, manipulation, deception and about how to make an opponent think you will do one thing when you intend to do something different. A poker player, a spin bowler, a tennis player all succeed through such means. Primary teachers would normally judge such qualities in children as morally dubious, even if they recognise that they require intelligence, skill, force of will and an ability to read other people, attributes likely to be useful for children throughout their lives. Games, however, can allow for their positive expression in the classroom by framing these qualities as virtues.

There is always, too, that element of chance in games, another characteristic of life that schools often find uncomfortable as they want to encourage children to think they can control their own destinies. Dice games and board games, such as 'Ludo', 'Snakes and Ladders' and 'Monopoly' allow children deliberately to play with chance and to experience the 'slings and arrows' of fortune in a less outrageous manner.

In Shakespeare's plays there are many examples of people taking sides and working together to defeat an opponent, such as Brutus, Cassius and the rest of the conspirators; and of people displaying individual skill and intelligence in order to win the day, such as Henry V or Portia in *The Merchant of Venice*. There are also plenty of people, such as Iago, who manipulate and deceive others in order to achieve their wicked aims. Games can allow children to explore the darker as well as the lighter side of human desires and behaviour and to experience the vagaries of chance or fate, so vividly expressed in plays such as *A Midsummer Night's Dream* and *Hamlet*. Such experiences can feel thrilling and even naughty at times but this is integral to their enjoyment. Games can, therefore, provide for children a safely distanced and enjoyable way to empathise and talk about the broad range of Shakespeare's moral universe.

Games help us celebrate being alive together

Some of Shakespeare's most famous lines are those in which characters ponder the nature and meaning of existence, often in a tragic voice. Think of Macbeth as he compares life to a 'tale told by an idiot, full of sound and fury, signifying nothing'. Or Hamlet in his famous soliloquy 'To be or not to be', in which he considers what, if anything, lies beyond death.

Yet there is a paradox here. Despite the bleakness of their subject matter, the plays are, at one and the same time, a glorious celebration of life. The actors are vibrant, charismatic, energetic, full of life, using language at its most expressive and powerfully beautiful. At the end of even the most tragic of his plays we are moved but also strangely uplifted. We feel glad to be alive.

Just stop and think for a minute, what a biological miracle it is that any of us are alive at all, least of all alive at the same time as everyone else around us. Sometimes it is good just to celebrate this miracle; and dancing, going to the theatre and playing together are some of the ways in which we do this. High-energy games in which they run, chase, laugh, touch and hug one another are a joyful way for the children in your class to celebrate their 'aliveness' and feel good together. Such feelings can form the foundation for the kind of ensemble work that recognises that Shakespeare is for everyone, not just the privileged, the academically gifted or the super-confident. It is this spirit of the ensemble, a spirit of togetherness, that underpins the pedagogic approaches that follow throughout this book.

The rest of this chapter outlines a range of games that have been grouped under different headings to indicate how they can fit in with your teaching of Shakespeare. However, these headings are simple guides and you can use the games flexibly. They can be adapted and changed to fit with a range of different plays, characters, conflicts and dilemmas. Some of these possibilities are indicated, others you will no doubt discover for yourself.

Games to build ensemble

'Go/stop together'

Children spread out in the space. When the teacher says 'Go', they move around the room, exploring as much of it as possible, keeping their distance from other children. When you say 'Stop' they are to stop and remain absolutely still until you say 'Go' again. The challenge is for them to try to go and stop at exactly the same time and to walk at exactly the same pace as everyone else.

- With younger children, walk with them and ask them to move/stop with you and to walk at your pace, which you can vary, of course.
- With older children, you might play the game in silence, providing them with the challenge of sensing the moment for them to move and stop together.
- You can add additional instructions for them to carry out in unison, such as clap, jump or shout 'My lord!' as you call them out.

'Huggy'

The above game can also lead straight into 'Huggy', in which you call out 'Huggy 4' or 'Huggy 5' and children get themselves into group hugs of that number with the children who happen to be closest to them. This can be a good way to make use of chance to get children into groups that they normally would not choose and hence get used to working with a range of others.

There are often a small number of children left over in a round of 'Huggy'. For example, if you call 'Huggy 4' and there are 26 children in the class, then two will not find a group. You can tell children that, if this happens, different groups can invite individuals left over to 'hide' inside their hug in a way that the teacher cannot spot them – but only to do this at the end, when it is clear that there are children left over.

'Show me a ...'

Once in groups, children can be invited to make a group image that in some way suggests the subject matter, characters, theme or setting of the play with which you are working. This is a particularly good game to play at the beginning of a project. With younger children about to work on *A Midsummer Night's Dream* you might call 'Show me some naughty fairies' or even 'Show me a forest'. To introduce *Julius Caesar* to older children you might say 'Show me a great leader'. If children are in groups of five, this means that four of them will need to show how they think people respond to this great leader.

- It helps if you give a countdown '5, 4, 3, 2, 1' so children do not discuss too much. They need to work quickly and think with their bodies.
- Do four or five of these images. You might comment yourself or invite children to comment on the different things they show you – what the various naughty fairies appear to be doing, for example, or the contrasting types of leader we are being shown.
- You might on occasion invite the tableaux to come spontaneously to life at a given word – but only for a few seconds, just to explore their possibilities.

'Clap your hands and pass it on'

You and the children stand in a circle. You turn quickly to the child on your left and clap your hands at them. They do the same to the child on their left and so on round the circle until the clap reaches you. You then send it back, this time to the child on your right. The game thus concludes when the clap has been passed round the circle twice, first one way then the other.

- Repeat the game, this time challenging the children to play it faster.
- Play it on your hands and knees. This time each of your hands slaps the floor one after the other. Otherwise the same rules apply.
- Add an emotion to the game. Clap fiercely with a stern face; or merrily with a broad smile; or stupidly with an idiotic face. If applicable, children can be invited to play it as a particular character might – for example, as Malvolio (sternly) or as Sir Andrew Aguecheek (idiotically) if you are working on *Twelfth Night*.

'Who speaks next?'

Take a couple of lines from a play you have been working with and that children are already very familiar with and make sure they know them and can say them together. The class stands in a circle and the object of the game is for the class to complete saying the lines out loud by individuals volunteering one word at a time, without signalling or putting their hands up. If two children speak at once then they have to start the lines again. Children, therefore, need to watch and listen to one another carefully.

- With younger children, take one line only.
- You can add an additional challenge by starting again if one child utters the wrong word.
- You may well wish to time how long it takes and have a cut-off point of, say, three minutes. Keep note of the time and challenge the children each time you play to see if they can beat their previous record.

'Find your twin'

Children stand in a space as you hand out cards to each of them. These cards provide them with a gesture and/or a line or phrase of greeting uttered by a character. So, if you were working on *Richard III*, a card might say 'Narrow your eyes, give a false smile and say "Brother, good day"' (which are the words Richard uses to greet Clarence in Act I). Another might say 'Frown, point angrily and cry out "What black magician conjures up this fiend?"' (which is how Anne greets Richard a scene later). They are told that one other person in the class has been given the same card as them. At a given word they are to move around the class and greet one another with their gesture and/or line until they have successfully found their twin.

Children can be told that, if they find their twin early, they are to practise making their gesture and saying their line in unison, as identically as possible, until the rest of the class has finished.

- The younger the class, the simpler the instructions on the card should be.
- Children can be asked after the game to reflect on what the line/gesture suggests about the character.
- This is a particularly apt game for those plays, such as *Twelfth Night* and *A Comedy of Errors*, where identical twins are central to the unfolding of the plot.

'Mirroring'

This is another game that works well with the theme of twins. Children are divided into pairs and asked to face one another. One child takes the lead and the other follows in performing a series of actions, which might be abstract or which might mime a common activity like washing one's face and cleaning one's teeth. They are to try to do these in absolute unison.

- The actions can be extended to moving in space – can they walk in the same way, for example, at the same pace, with the same gait?
- Children might briefly rehearse these movements and then show them to the class. Can we tell them apart or is one definitely leading?

'Yes, let's!'

This is a game for older primary children to play in groups of about six. First of all, discuss the things that a particular character does in the play you are studying and make a list of at least six of them. So, if the character is Richard III, the list might include pretending to be nice to people while secretly plotting to kill them; seeing the ghost of someone you have had murdered; and losing and searching for your horse in battle. Then, standing in a circle in their groups, the children number themselves 1 to 6 and are told that this is the space they are to work in throughout the game. As you call out 'Number 1', this child is to jump into the circle and call out something from the list with great enthusiasm: 'I know, let's all lose our horse in battle and go round looking for it!' The rest of the group call out 'Yes, let's!' and spontaneously act out doing just that until you call out the next number and the game continues.

Games to physicalise the world of the play

'Go, stop, show me ...'

Children walk through the space on the word 'Go'. They are then asked to stop and show a character from the play you are studying together. Rather than just call out the name, use a descriptive phrase taken from the text itself. So, for *The Tempest*, you might call out, 'Show me the Duke of Milan, "a prince of power"'; for Caliban, 'Show me "a freckled whelp, hag born, not honoured with a human shape"'.

'Exit pursued by a bear'

Children walk through space until you call stop. You then give them an instruction on an exit or entrance taken directly from the text. 'Exit pursued by a bear' is a famous stage direction from *The Winter's Tale*. Others from the same play could include 'Enter surrounded by guards'; 'Exit with ladies and attendants'; 'Enter, singing'; 'Exit Clown'; 'Enter, dancing, with twelve rustics dressed like satyrs'. The game is best played if children are asked spontaneously to adopt any of the characters involved in the exit/entrance but to respond quickly. So, if someone decides to be a bear and starts pursuing me, I shouldn't decide that I am a bear, too!

'Guided tours'

Children are asked to imagine the details of a particular setting, such as the island in *The Tempest*, the Greek camp in *Troilus and Cressida* or the castle of Elsinore in *Hamlet*. They are given individual sheets of A4 paper and marker pens to write and/or draw what they imagine they can see, hear and smell. These are then spread around the space to make a 'word (or image) carpet'. Children then get into pairs. A is then asked to close their eyes while B is to lead them on a guided tour around the space, using the details provided on the word carpet to describe what they can see and hear. You can model for 30 seconds how to do this. 'Right now be careful here. There are some narrow steps leading down into a dungeon. Uuurgggh! Can you smell the damp and the dirt down here? Has somebody died?' etc. After a couple of minutes, stop the game and ask the children to share some of the most memorable features of the tour so far. Partners can then change roles with the new guide being asked to be even more evocative in their detail than the first.

Games of power

'Fair is foul and foul is fair'

In *The Taming of the Shrew*, Petruchio refuses to feed his new wife Kate until she absolutely bends to his will. One of his tests is to get her to agree to whatever he says, pointing at the moon and insisting that she calls it the sun, for example. This is an extreme form of bullying, the kind of behaviour children instinctively find unfair. There are various ways that you can play with this idea to explore the extremes of the master/slave or master/servant relationships that occur in different plays (Prospero and Caliban, for example).

- You can play 'Stop/Go', insisting that the children stop when you say 'Go' and go when you say 'Stop'. If you vary the pace and speed at which you do this, it can become very tricky. If you have a child take the role of teacher you can ask them how it makes them feel to have the power to change the meaning of words for their classmates!
- Children can play a game that uses some of the words that Petruchio and Kate use in Act IV, Scene 5. A begins by playing the master and B the slave and they alternate roles with each exchange, trying to be more outrageous each time. The exchange proceeds in the following manner:

A: Look (pointing to a pen, or a window, or a boy), 'tis a book (a door/a girl).
B: A book? No, my lord, 'tis a pen!
A: I say it is a book.
B: Henceforth I vow it shall be so for me.

'Prospero's coming'

This is a game based on 'Captain's coming!'. The teacher takes on the role of Prospero and calls out a range of jobs for Caliban (the children) to do:

Caliban, gather the logs – come on, quicker, you lazy creature. They don't look heavy enough to me – pick up more, go on, more! Let me see you sweat and pant as you carry some of those heavy ones. Now bring them here and light my fire. I am cold and I want you to cook my dinner.

And so on, being as mean as you like. Afterwards the children talk about how Caliban must feel being treated like that.

A version of this can be played in pairs, with each child being given a minute to make the other do as many horrible and difficult jobs as possible. They can then discuss which role they prefer, master or slave, and why.

'Antipholus says ...'

This is a version of 'Simon says ...' and derives its name from the two masters, both identical twins, in *The Comedy of Errors* (see Chapter 3). Children are cast as the servant, Dromio, and given various instructions to carry out, but they should only do so when the instructions are preceded by the phrase 'Antipholus says'.

In the play, both sets of masters and servants are not only identical but have identical names. The game can reflect this and be made more complicated – and hence more fun – if there are two sets of Dromios in the class. The teacher has two different hats to help the children recognise which Antipholus is their master. They should only respond to the commands of their own master and only when he says 'Antipholus says'!

Games of conflict and aggression

'Shakespeare sets you free!'

This is a chase game that can be adapted to many plays. Two of the children are chasers, the rest of the children are being chased. If the chaser touches a child they have to freeze and stay still until they are set free. In order for this to happen another child has to touch them and say a given line or phrase from the play in question before they are released. So, for example, if Malvolio is chasing Olivia through the garden in *Twelfth Night*, then the line might be 'Some have greatness thrust upon 'em!'; if Hermia and Helena are chasing Demetrius and Lysander (or vice versa) through the woods in *A Midsummer Night's Dream*, the line can be Puck's 'If we shadows have offended / Think but this and all is mended'. Children can be given the challenge to see how many they can set free, as well as how long they can stay free themselves.

'Caesar, Brutus, Mark Anthony'

This is a version of 'Scissors, paper, stone'. Children offer ideas for a frozen image of each of the three characters that are recognisably different in shape and level. So Caesar might be tall and proud, as if waving from a horse; Brutus might be thrusting a dagger; Mark Anthony might be stooped, carrying Caesar's body. These need to be agreed and practised in a version of 'Go, stop, show me ...'. Caesar beats Mark Anthony (as Mark Anthony always acknowledges him as his leader); Mark Anthony beats Brutus (as he tricks and eventually defeats him in battle); Brutus beats Caesar (as he kills him).

- Children can be asked to discuss who should beat whom from their knowledge of the play, rather than your simply telling them.
- This can be played as a team game, with each team agreeing in secrecy which character they will be. Then the teams line up facing each other from opposite walls. As you count they take a step closer to one another – '1, 2, 3 and *Show*!' – whereupon they are to freeze immediately into their character. If they decide they have lost they must run back to the safety of their own wall; if they have won they can try to capture a member of the opposite team by touching them before they reach their wall. If they manage this, then the captive changes sides for the next round. The game continues for four or five rounds or until one side has clearly won.
- The game could similarly be played with the characters of Macbeth, Macduff and Duncan; or to reflect the many love triangles we find in Shakespeare's plays, such as *A Midsummer Night's Dream* and *Twelfth Night*.

'Caliban's footsteps'

Like in the game 'Grandmother's footsteps', the class (Caliban) tries to creep up on the teacher (Prospero) while you have your back turned and they must freeze when you turn round to look. If you see anyone moving, you point at them and shout 'Abhorred slave! Hag seed, hence!'. Children do not have to return if the class can call back to you with the words 'This island's mine! Toads, beetles, bats, light on you!'.

'Do you bite your thumb, sir?'

Children spread out in space. At your word they run around until you call out 'Freeze!' at which point they are to freeze in an exaggerated, aggressive posture, look someone in the eye and, together, challenge them with this, or some other suitably aggressive insult/phrase from the text of the play you are studying. They then pull a face at them and blow a loud raspberry before running around again and the game continues for four or five turns.

- Ask children to freeze each time in a different posture, varying in level and shape, making their face look increasingly aggressive each time.
- Specify with whom they are to make eye contact – someone very close to them, for example, or someone at the other side of the room;
- Play the game in a much more understated, menacing manner. This time children walk through the space, stopping and holding eye contact with someone as you call 'Freeze!' Try to say this in a low, threatening voice. They are to convey aggression only through their eyes and the tension in their body, saying the line in a low, menacing tone, holding the eye contact until you give the word, trying, above all things, not to laugh until you invite them to move on.

'Verbal tennis'

This is a good game to play before tackling a dialogue which consists of the kind of ripostes we saw earlier between Hamlet and his mother or the menace underlying the exchange between Hector and Achilles in *Troilus and Cressida* (see Chapter 2). It is played in pairs. A is to say two words, B is to respond with their opposite; for example, 'Come, come!/Go, go!'; 'Come here/stay there'; 'I answer/you question'. You can model this by playing it with the whole class first.

- Play it miming a tennis game, saying the words as you mime striking the ball.
- Play it with a smile or a frown – your partner is to respond with the opposite.

'Finger fencing'

A game for pairs. Each player stands facing their opponent. Each has their left arm behind them, pressing their hand into the small of their back, fingers spread, palm facing outward. The object of the game is to stab your opponent in the palm of their left hand with the forefinger of your right hand, at which point you call out 'A hit! A palpable hit!' (*Hamlet*) and the game starts again.

It is best played with a Shakespearean insult at the start of each round – there are many, many of these to be found in every play. Each player faces the other and 'draws their sword', calling out an insult such as 'Thou liest, thou cheating monkey thou!' (*Romeo and Juliet*) or 'Do you bandy looks with me, you rascal?' (*King Lear*) before engaging.

'Sword and shield'

Children walk in space and are secretly to choose one child whom they are to imagine is a sword attempting to kill them and another who is a shield protecting them. They are to try to keep the shield between themselves and the sword at all times. At the end of the game they can be asked to name anyone they think was using them as either a sword or shield.

'We do but keep the peace!'

This is a game for older children. Two children are chosen as the peacekeepers and the rest of the class are given different lines from the play you are studying, all of which need to be spoken in a loud, heated, aggressive manner. The two peace-keepers stand in space, smiling and gently waving as children, rapidly and in turn, come up as close as possible to them, looking as aggressive as they like, calling out their lines with as much menace as they can muster. The only rule is that they must not touch either of the peacekeepers in any way, whose job it is to keep smiling, keep waving and after each threat say together 'We do but keep the peace!'.

Those children who prove to be good at being peacekeepers can discuss their tactics for staying calm in the face of so much aggression.

'Trust me, I'm an actor!' – games of deception and disguise

'The poisoned pearl'

The class sits in a circle, with one child in the centre. The poisoned pearl (a marble) is being passed around from hand to hand in front of their eyes ... or is it? At any point a child may decide to keep it and only pretend to pass it on. But it is the job of those in the circle not to make this obvious. When the teacher calls a halt to the game the child in the centre is called upon to accuse someone of having the poisoned pearl. They can be given up to three guesses. Alternatively, the child can be invited to halt the game at any time they think they know who has the pearl and can be given up to three chances to guess correctly.

'Wink murder'

Children stand in space and close their eyes. The teacher selects a child by touching them on the shoulder. This child knows they are the murderer but no one else knows this. When the children open their eyes they are to move around in space. If anyone looks them in the face and winks at them they know that this is the murderer and they have just been killed. They are then to die loudly, calling out a suitable line from Shakespeare, agreed in advance, such as 'Et tu, Brute? Then fall Caesar' or Juliet's 'This is thy sheath: there rust, and let me die' or, for Hamlet, 'O, I die, Horatio – the rest is silence'. They then remove themselves to the side of the room and watch. The game can be halted at any time if a child thinks they have spotted the murderer at work. If they are right, the game can start again with a new murderer. The murderer, therefore, needs to go about their task very carefully so as not to be discovered – a good game to play before dealing with the murder of Duncan in *Macbeth*.

'Hector's dilemma'

This game is a good way to begin work on *Troilus and Cressida*. Divide the class into two camps and explain that they represent two armies, each of which has been brought up to fight honourably. The problem is, honour isn't winning the war and each day both sides are faced with the same dilemma; should they fight according to the rules, and let the war drag on, or fight dirty with the aim of winning it quickly?

Each army begins the game with 100 men and is given two large cards with the words 'honourably' and 'dishonourably' written on them. The armies discuss in a huddle and decide which card to play. If they decide to fight cleanly (honourably) and their opponents do, too, each gains ten men. If each decides to fight dirty (dishonourably), both armies lose ten men. If one fights clean and the other dirty, then the cheats win – they gain ten men and the other army loses ten men. Keep a running count of the scores and after a few rounds stop the game and declare which army, if any, is the winner.

The game can become even more interesting if you allow children to nominate a negotiator who meets with their opposite number to see if the armies can make an agreement for both to fight cleanly. Of course, there is always the danger that they will make this agreement but that one army will secretly renege on it. Don't point out this possibility but see if the children think of it themselves. Invariably, if this act of treachery produces a victory, the army that wins will cheer and the children will feel very pleased with themselves. That is fine … but you can, good naturedly, ask them why they are so proud of being cheats. Is winning more important than playing fairly? This can lead to a vigorous discussion as to whether war can ever be a fair thing; and whether fighting honourably is more important than winning or vice versa.

Word play

'The pentameter canter'

Shakespeare's poetry is most typically written using the iambic pentameter, lines of ten syllables, with the stress falling on the even syllable:

If **music** **be** the **food** of **love**, play **on**

Friends, **Ro**mans, **coun**trymen, lend **me** your **ears**!

There are various ways in which you can encourage children to play with this rhythm; by repeating the lines aloud after you, clapping on each stressed syllable, for example, or by tapping your right hand on your chest, like a heartbeat, as you say them together.

The pace and rhythm of the iambic pentameter adapts itself very readily to that of a cantering horse – just try it now; imagine you are in the saddle, holding the reins, and say the two lines above to the rhythm of the ride. Once children have a feel for this, they can be put into pairs and given a few famous lines to play with in the form of a canter around the space.

- You can have more fun, casting them as particular horse riders – as terribly posh or as cowboys, for example – and asking them to speak accordingly.
- It is quite easy to make up your own iambic pentameters in ordinary conversation as they echo so closely the pattern of everyday English speech. Try continuing this soliloquy for two lines or so, emphasising the iambic rhythm.

I wonder where I've left the register?
Oh no, it may be on the toilet floor!
No, surely not, I wouldn't leave it there …

- When they are used to it, older children can be given the challenge of having a conversation around a given theme in the form of the iambic pentameter, while out cantering with their friend! Allow for a pause between each cantering line for the partners to come up with a response.

'The text fills the space!'

Children stand in space and are given a line such as Richard III's 'A horse, a horse, my kingdom for a horse' or Malvolio's desperate plea in *Twelfth Night*: 'I am not mad, Sir Topas! I say to you this house is dark'. They are to call it out, repeatedly, from where they stand, directing it into every corner and angle of the room until you give the signal to stop.

'Chant/sing the names'

Names can often be organised into simple lines of music for you to sing and for children to echo. Young children particularly enjoy this. Possible examples from *The Tempest* are given below. Each line has a beat of four, which you can clap out with the children, with the vocal stress on the second and fourth beat in each, as marked.

Alon**so**, Anto**nio**, / both want **rid** of Pros**pe**ro
Ferdi**nand** or Cali**ban**? / Which one **is** Miranda's **man**?

'Vowels, nothing but vowels'

Choose a memorable line or two from the text the children have been working with and remove all of the consonants. Speak it out loud with the same intonation you would ordinarily use to give meaning to the phrase. Can the children work out what line it is? Once it has been recognised, have the children say the line out loud together with just the vowels. Exercises such as this can help to sensitise children to the musical qualities of the language.

'Kit's game'

This is a version of 'Kim's game', played only with lines from Shakespeare. Tell children that, early in his career, Shakespeare had a great rival, one Christopher or 'Kit' Marlowe who, as well as being a great playwright, got up to some pretty suspect behaviour. We are to imagine that this included sneaking into Will Shakespeare's study and deleting key words from lines in his plays that he had written the night before. Can we help Will here? Write a line or couplet from the text you have been working with on the board. Children read it before closing their eyes. Erase a word and see if anyone can remember which it is. Invite a child who thinks they know to write it in the space. Continue with further examples.

'Macbeth in the Marines'

We are all used to seeing American marines training in action movies, running in unison and echoing the lines chanted by their leader: 'We don't care what people say / Gonna whupp them anyway'. The opening lines of Macbeth can be readily adapted to scan perfectly for this.

> When shall we three meet again?
> In thunder, lightning, or in rain?
> When the hurlyburly's done,
> When the battle's lost and won.
> Fair is foul and foul is fair:
> Through the fog and filthy air.

Have the children line up behind you and lead them round the class, yourself in role as Macbeth in the Marines, they as his soldiers. Children will learn these lines very quickly and many will love taking the lead themselves when you play this again in later sessions.

Of course, it is the witches and not Macbeth who chant these lines; and such a representation would never be seen in a serious production of the play; but, as we pointed out in the introduction, in our teaching of Shakespeare, it is often important *not* to be earnest! And all kinds of games help us remember that!

Chapter 2

Beginning Shakespeare with his stories

Throughout this book we argue that Shakespeare's stories can be emotionally appealing and thought-provoking to children through their characters, plot lines, settings and through the kind of problems and issues that they address. One of the key means of interesting your class in his work, then, is to lure them into the world of his stories and to spend time together imaginatively living through them. Doing this actively through drama has several advantages over simply reading a written version of the tale:

- It will allow children to feel they are building the story together from within, rather than simply hearing someone else's version of it.
- It will help children to connect with the human issues and dilemmas that are the heartbeat of the plays, by acting and talking as if they were in the world of the play rather than observing and discussing it from the outside.
- Even when you and the class are not using the lines that Shakespeare wrote to explore the stories, you will be working within the art form in which he wrote them.

Storytelling strategies

One of the core advantages of working in the ways we propose in this book is the fact that they provide you with models – or metaphors – for being a teacher that are different from the norm and very motivating for children. So, in games you are a referee, arbitrating and making sure that the games are played fairly, something children respect and are happy to adhere to. Another form of authority that children will readily submit to is that of the storyteller. In *Beginning Drama 4–11* (2008), we discussed the importance of oral storytelling and how its physicality and immediacy make it a ready pedagogic tool for drama teaching. We also suggested that you might make use of a 'story stick' or 'story wand' to indicate to the children when you are taking on the role of storyteller. This can set up an immediate expectation that exciting and interesting things are about to start happening.

The idea of the story stick as a kind of magic wand introduces a third, powerful metaphor – that of the teacher as a magician who, like Prospero, can physically conjure up all kinds of worlds ; in this case, the world of one of Shakespeare's plays. A very good way of using the story wand is to have children sit in a circle while you playfully narrate a part of the plot which they spontaneously act out together.[1] This is a very fluid activity. Children need never take on a particular role for very long, as you will regularly utter a mysterious sound to clear the circle and so continue the story with new volunteers. Not only is this a highly active and enjoyable way for children to internalise important elements of the plot, it is also a way for you to introduce 'text scraps' – phrases drawn from the play itself to describe characters, places and deeds, or lines of dialogue that are particularly memorable or significant. Very importantly, the playful and improvisatory spirit of this activity – sometimes called a 'Whoosh', after the mysterious sound the teacher makes to clear the circle – encourages the spirit of the ensemble, as children work unselfconsciously with those who happen to be in the circle with them.

There is a delicate balancing act for the teacher when encouraging children to experience the world of the play from within. We want to grant children enough creative freedom so that they feel their ideas matter while, at the same time, knowing that we cannot break away from the storyline itself without turning the drama into something that isn't Shakespeare's. To make use of Philip Pullman's phrase, we need to remember that 'the story always wins'. In this sense, we can think of our drama as a series of alluring play areas, all of which offer different challenges and points of interest for the children, with clear boundaries and fences to keep us together and stop anyone from wandering off and getting lost. Sometimes we can jump over the fence from one area into the next but often you, the teacher, will need to lead the children there along a pathway, itself very interesting and exciting. The pathway is the storyline, where the teacher assumes the role of guide, of storyteller, with a story whose details, characters and underlying meanings are played with, lingered on, delved into and explored in the play areas you lead them to, through the drama activities you set up for them.

Selecting storylines

There are certain stories from Shakespeare that are generally considered to be most suitable for young children, often for very superficial reasons – *A Midsummer Night's Dream*, for example, because it has fairies in it. We have hinted so far, however, that many of the plays, even those considered to be difficult and adult, can be of great interest to children, provided we approach them from a perspective on the world that children will readily understand. Once children are hooked into the story, we can trust the play's complexity to broaden these perspectives, thus educating them in the truest sense of the word.

There is another challenge for the teacher, however. The plays are long, the characters numerous, the plotlines hardly ever simple, the action spread across various settings, usually with sub-plots that reflect or offer an ironic contrast to the main plot. What you need to do, then, is to select a through-line; decide which characters and aspects of the plot you will weave your own version of the drama around. Depending upon the play and the age of your children, you can be brutally selective – but your intention should be, as far as possible, to remain true to the spirit of the play by having a clear idea as to how this section of the story will interest your children; and – crucially – what you hope it will make them feel and think about. Remember, Shakespeare didn't tell stories to teach moral lessons; but he did tell them to provoke, to move, to make his audiences think and wonder about the world they all lived in.

For the rest of this chapter we will outline two examples, deliberately choosing plays that might not initially spring to mind as suitable for primary-aged children. First, we will look at how we can adapt *The Winter's Tale* for lower juniors and then move on to a longer scheme for upper juniors around a play that has often been seen as particularly challenging and problematic, *Troilus and Cressida*.

Before you make use of either of these or of any of the examples we present in this book, a few points need to be kept in mind:

- You should make sure you read the play first and, if possible, watch a version of it, whether live or on DVD.
- Some of the activities will be suitable for work in the classroom, others will require you to be in a larger space, such as the school hall.
- The examples are not presented as lesson plans, so you will need to adapt them, perhaps including games to make sure the rhythm of activities is right, so that children are not kept sitting for too long.
- Where suggestions are made for working with text, ideas on how to go about this can be found in Chapter 4.
- There are plenty of possibilities for developing writing from this work and many of these are suggested and outlined in Chapter 5.

Lower KS2 – *The Winter's Tale*

A winter's tale in Shakespeare's time was a fairy tale to be told around a winter's fire and there are recognisable elements in it that resonate with fairy tales still popular today. A jealous and foolish king orders his baby daughter to be taken out and abandoned; she is found and eventually grows into a beautiful young woman who marries a handsome prince. Like a fairy tale, the story begins unhappily and quickly gets worse when a mother and daughter are cruelly separated, but ends happily with a marriage, redemption for the king and the promise of future good fortune for all. As such, it is a story that young children can connect with quite readily. The scheme presented below demonstrates how a very simple structure of making key images can help children create and understand the arc of the play's storyline in a straightforward, efficient and collaborative manner.

Begin with a game of 'Go, stop, show me …' (see Chapter 1, page 13) to cover ideas such as friendship, jealousy, love and being a prisoner. Finally, ask children a difficult one: 'Show me truth'. Just go along with what the children give you here and talk about what they show, asking them to explain why. The real learning will occur in such unpacking and discussion of their ideas. Having talked about truth, you can introduce the idea of the Oracle. If your class has done any previous work on Ancient Greece, they may already have heard of this, of course. You can always bring home the power of the Oracle by asking them to imagine, if you had one in school, to whom it might be very useful and what kind of questions it might be asked.

Now play a game of 'Exit pursued by a bear' before putting the children into groups and asking them to make the images listed below. When you do this:

- start by asking them to make a still image;
- then ask them to introduce some brief action that moves into another still image (*still – move – still*), one that still represents the theme they have been given;
- then give each group their lines written on card and ask them to include these in some way. Encourage the children to be imaginative and playful here, using selected phrases or words, for example, and repeating them, or speaking them chorally, perhaps.

Once the first six images are ready, have the class perform and share them, encouraging speculation about the story. Then, and only then, should you add in the narrative links, presented in the boxes below. These are quite minimal and, although you could read them as written, if you feel more confident as a storyteller, it would be better to use them to create more vivid narrative links of your own. When you are naming each character in your narration, it is a good idea to indicate which is which in the image, to help ease the children's understanding.

Image 1: Friends from boyhood

Camillo: I think there is not in this world either malice or matter can alter this.

> There were once two kings; King Leontes of Sicily and King Polixenes of Bohemia. They were great friends and had been so since they were boys. Each also had a son – Leontes' son was called Mamillius and Polixenes' son was called Florizel.

Image 2: A jealous husband suspects his friend

Leontes: My heart dances, but not for joy, not for joy.
Hermione: He something seems unsettled.

Now King Polixenes had been staying happily with his great friend, as he often did. When it was time for him to go, Leontes asked him if he would like to stay longer, but Polixenes declined. So Leontes asked his wife, Queen Hermione, to try to persuade his friend not to leave. When she managed to do this quite easily, Leontes immediately grew jealous and convinced himself that there must be something going on between his wife and his friend. In fact, his jealousy quickly became so strong that he even resolved to have his best friend murdered and ordered his loyal servant, Camillo, to do the wicked deed.

Image 3: A plot to murder is given away

Camillo: I am appointed to murder you.
Polixenes: By whom, Camillo?
Camillo: By the king. He thinks that you have touched his queen forbiddenly.

But Camillo could not bring himself to obey Leontes and so he told Polixenes of the king's murderous plan. They both decided to run away together to Bohemia, where Polixenes was, of course, king. Meanwhile Queen Hermione was expecting a baby and, in his madness, Leontes had begun to believe that the child was not his! Convinced that his wife had been unfaithful to him, he had her locked up in a prison.

Image 4: A king rejects his baby daughter

Leontes: My child? Away with't! Take it hence and see it instantly consumed by fire!
Antigonus: I'll pawn the little blood which I have left to save the innocent.
Leontes: Let it live. Carry this female bastard hence to some remote and barren place quite out of our dominions.

When the baby was born, Leontes told his friend, the faithful Lord Antigonus, to take her and leave her, abandoned, far away from his kingdom. With the child in his care, Antigonus set off and sailed away in a ship. While on board the ship, he slept and Queen Hermione appeared to him in a dream, telling him to take the baby girl to Bohemia and to name her Perdita, which means 'lost girl'.

Image 5: A queen is accused and the Oracle is consulted

Hermione: I do refer me to the Oracle. Apollo be my judge.
Leontes: There is no truth at all in the Oracle. This is mere falsehood.

Back in Sicily, Queen Hermione was put on trial, wrongly accused of being unfaithful to her husband. In order to prove her innocence, she asked for the Oracle to be consulted. This was done and the Oracle confirmed that she was indeed telling the truth. However, Leontes, her husband, refused to believe it. No sooner had he announced this refusal to the entire court than a servant arrived with the news that Mamillus, his son, who had been sick, had died. On hearing this, and as a result of all that had happened to her, the queen became so distressed that she collapsed. Her good and loyal friend, Paulina, told the king that she was dead and that he was responsible for her death! Only then did Leontes come to his senses and he vowed to mourn the death of his wife and son every day for the rest of his life.

Image 6: Exit pursued by a bear

Antigonous: I am gone for ever!
Old shepherd: What have we here? Mercy on's, a bairn. A very pretty bairn.

Meanwhile, on the shores of Bohemia, Antigonus arrived with the baby girl, Perdita. But he was immediately attacked and killed by a bear, thus leaving the child alone. Fortunately, an old shepherd saw what happened and rescued the child. Beside her he found a box which had in it more gold than the shepherd could ever have dreamed of – he called it fairy gold! The box also had papers in it that related Perdita's story. The shepherd, however, was unable to read so did not know what they were about. He decided to take the child home and raise her as his own.

At this moment in the play, roughly halfway through, Shakespeare introduces Time in the form of a chorus. Experiment with different ways of bringing Time to life and ask the children how they might show this much time – 16 whole years – passing on stage. Also ask why Shakespeare might have chosen to use this device.

Time passes

Chorus: Now take upon me in the name of Time
         To use my wings. Impute it not a crime
         To me or my swift passage that I slide
         O'er sixteen years and leave the growth untried

These 16 years of untold story can be seen as a space for the children to speculate about what might have happened. What sort of a place do they imagine Bohemia to be? You can create the landscape with them by, for instance, using a word carpet like the one we use to create the island from *The Tempest* in Chapter 3 – where does King Polixenes live? Where might the old shepherd live? What sort of things would the shepherd's 'daughter' have to learn? Building on what they have done before, the children's ideas can be created as mini scenes using the *still – move – still* structure described earlier. They can then discuss a possible order for these ideas and perform them as a continuous, linked narrative of Perdita's childhood.

You are now ready to move on to create the remaining images and tell the rest of the story.

Image 7: A king in disguise to spy on his son

Polixenes:	(To Camillo) This is the prettiest low-born lass that ever ran on greensward.
	(To Florizel) Have you a father?
Florizel:	I have. But what of him?
Polixenes:	Knows he of this?
Florizel:	He neither does nor shall.

> In Bohemia, Polixenes' son, Florizel, had also grown up in the intervening 16 years. By chance, Florizel met Perdita one day and the two fell in love. But Florizel kept his true identity secret and when he went to the old shepherd to ask for Perdita's hand in marriage, he used a different name. What he did not know, however, was that his father, King Polixenes, had become suspicious about the way he was spending all of his time with this shepherd girl. So, along with his faithful servant, Camillo (remember him?), the king disguised himself and followed Florizel. When he discovered what was going on, and that Florizel wanted to marry this girl, he was so furious that he instantly disinherited him, saying he would no longer regard him as his son.

Image 8: Running away in secret

Florizel:	Fortune speed us!
	Thus we set on, Camillo, to th' seaside.
Camillo:	The swifter speed the better.

> Camillo, however, did not agree with his master's hasty decision and made a plan to help the two young lovers. Secretly he led them to a boat that then set sail for Sicily. Sicily, you will remember, is where Perdita had been born and where her true father, Leontes, was still king. Camillo then told Polixenes that his son and his true love had left the country but the king vowed to pursue them, once more taking Camillo with him. The shepherd, too, set off in pursuit of Perdita, taking with him the papers that could prove who she really was.

Image 9: Friends, fathers and children re-united

Gentleman: There might you have beheld one joy crown another. Our king, being ready to leap out of himself for joy of his found daughter, asks Bohemia forgiveness, then embraces his son-in-law.

Once back in Sicily, Perdita and Florizel went straight to King Leontes to ask for his help and protection. Hot on their heels came King Polixenes, Camillo and the old shepherd. When Perdita's real identity was then revealed, everyone could be happy. Leontes had found his daughter, Polixenes could see that his son was actually marrying a princess! What is more, she was the daughter of his old friend, who was now truly sorry for all of the bad things he had done in the past.

Image 10: A statue of the dead queen comes to life

Polixenes: Masterly done.
                The very life seems warm upon her lip.
Leontes: Hermione was not so much wrinkled, nothing so agèd as this seems.
                (Hermione slowly descends)
Leontes: O, she's warm!
                If this be magic, let it be an art lawful as eating.

Queen Hermione's faithful servant, Paulina, had stayed with Leontes through all the intervening years. And now she had a big surprise for him! She took him to see a statue of the long-dead queen which was uncannily life-like. As Leontes approached it, the statue seemed to be breathing. As he stood there, admiring and wondering at it, he was suddenly amazed to see it come to life. In fact, it was no statue at all but the true queen whom he had wronged all those years before. Now that he was truly sorry and had suffered for his misdeeds, Paulina had decided that he and his queen could be re-united. So Perdita and Florizel married, as did Camillo and Paulina! And, as with all good winter's tales, everyone lived happily ever after.

Upper KS2 – *Troilus and Cressida*

Troilus and Cressida presents a vision of the Homeric world at odds with the usual heroic way in which it is portrayed. It centres upon that part of the Trojan War that we hear of in Homer's *Iliad*, in which Achilles has quarrelled with Agamemnon, but its action finishes before the fall of Troy itself. Achilles is presented in a particularly unflattering manner, as lazy, arrogant, boorish and a cheat in battle. Hector, his adversary in Troy, is seen in a more sympathetic light, as essentially honourable but swept along by family quarrels and forces of political cynicism and treachery that he cannot control. These are, then, a very human and flawed bunch of heroes, locked in a war that no one seems able to win. In the midst of this action there is a love affair between Troilus, Hector's youngest brother and one of the princes of Troy, and Cressida, whose father has long since sided with the Greeks and now lives in their camp. She has been left in the protection of her uncle, Pandarus, a figure of dubious moral principles who conspires to persuade her and Troilus to become lovers, only to see her immediately traded to the Greeks by Priam, the father of Troilus, in exchange for a Trojan hostage. Cressida is escorted to the camp by the Greek soldier, Diomedes, and once there quickly becomes his lover. The reasons for this are never clarified but there is a hint that, as a beautiful woman in a camp full of hostile soldiers, she sees him as a protector. Troilus learns of her infidelity to him and determines to kill Diomedes in battle. We never see whether he manages this; instead, we see his elder brother, Hector, unarmed, butchered by Achilles and a gang of his thugs. The last time we see Troilus, he is uttering words full of vengeance, hatred and despair. They are also heavily ironic, as we know that he and his city will soon be destroyed.

This is an edited and selective version of the story around which the scheme of work presented below has been planned. It has been chosen for the following reasons:

- Many children study the Greeks as part of their KS2 curriculum. If this scheme is taught in the light of such a project, they will be aware of the context and background of this story.
- Although tales of the heroes have great mythic power, it is good to offer other perspectives on their violent actions. This is particularly the case when children are old enough to understand and therefore ponder the fact that concepts such as good and evil are seldom as simple as many popular stories would have us believe.
- The play raises many themes that children of this age will generally have a strong interest in: when is something worth fighting over? What makes a fair fight? Why do people you love sometimes break their promises and betray your trust? Why do you do that yourself sometimes? What happens when powerful people are arrogant, stupid and big-headed? What happens when parents fail to take account of their children's feelings?[2]
- There is something here for those children who like love stories and for those who like war stories and the plot skilfully inter-relates the two, so that they become inseparable. The story will, then, get girls talking about war and boys talking about love, thus working against gender stereotyping.

Introductory activities

Gather the children into a circle and place two visual symbols, one of love and one of war, interlocked in its centre – a white veil or a wedding photograph with a wooden sword or dagger, perhaps. Ask the children to discuss what these signs might tell us about the story we are going to work on together. You can then ask them to raise their hands if they like love stories and again if they like war stories, so enabling you to point out that this story will have something of interest for all of them.

If it has been some time since the class has studied the Greeks, a brief revision exercise of the causes and progress of the Trojan War will be helpful. A simple way to do this is to divide the class into groups of three or four and to give each group a card with a number on one side and a sentence on the other. Each group is to read out the sentence they have been given while presenting a still image they have made to illustrate it. The numbers on the cards indicate the order for this. The example presented below will suit you if you have a class of 30 with fairly good levels of literacy.

1 Paris was a prince of Troy and the most handsome man in the world. Aphrodite, the goddess of love, told him he would one day marry the most beautiful woman in the world.
2 The most beautiful woman in the world was called Helen and she was married to a Greek prince called Menelaus.
3 Paris stole the beautiful Helen from her husband and together they fled back to his own city, Troy.
4 Prince Menelaus was furious at having his wife stolen from him and asked his brother, the powerful Prince Agamemnon, for help.
5 Agamemnon called all the princes of Greece together and ordered a huge fleet of ships to be built.
6 The Greek army then sailed across the sea to Troy.
7 Once the Greeks reached Troy, they camped outside the walls and laid siege to the city.
8 The siege of Troy dragged on for years with neither side able to win the war.

These sentences can be readily adapted to suit the numbers and ability levels of your class. You could, for example, include at the beginning details about the quarrel over the golden apple on Mount Olympus that lay behind Aphrodite's promise to Paris. If you think it useful, you can show the images again without the commentary and ask the children in each group to retell it together in their own words. If the children have never heard the story of the Trojan War, we suggest that you cover this briefly first as a separate topic, perhaps in your literacy work.

Setting the scene

The game 'Hector's dilemma', described in Chapter 1 on page 18, is a good way to establish the moral climate of the play, as the point system in this version has been deliberately skewed to make cheating seem like the best way to gain victory. Children can be asked afterwards whether they think anyone on either side might be tempted to fight dirty after being in stalemate for so long.

Children can now explore the two worlds of the play – the Greek camp and the city of Troy (also known as Ilium) – by playing 'Guided tours', as described in Chapter 1, page 13.

It is now time for children to meet some of the main characters. Put them into six groups and give each group a card with the name and brief description of a key character from Troy, as follows (the Greek characters are introduced into the story later). Ask each group to make an image to illustrate and accompany the reading of this card.

- *Hector:* the oldest of the princes; proud, brave and the commander of the Trojan forces.
- *Troilus:* the youngest of the princes; brave, handsome but with a quick temper.
- *Helen:* by reputation the most beautiful woman in the world.
- *Cressida:* a young woman whom many think to be as beautiful as Helen.
- *Pandarus:* an old, scheming uncle who wants his niece to find a rich boy-friend.
- *Cassandra:* a rather wild princess who predicts future disaster for Troy.

You will by now have set the scene sufficiently for the story to begin. As in the example of *The Winter's Tale*, the boxed words throughout the scheme are those you might use yourself in the role of storyteller.

Our story begins: Pandarus arranges a date

These were dark days in Troy. The war had been dragging on for many years and old uncle Pandarus was worried. He had been looking after his niece, Cressida, ever since her father – his brother – had switched sides to go and live in the Greek camp. That was some years ago and Cressida had since grown into a beautiful young woman – some people said she was as beautiful as Helen herself. So Pandarus had decided it was time to find a good love match for her – and who better than Troilus, the youngest of the princes of Troy, whom many thought to be the most handsome prince of them all? Now Troilus had seen Cressida from a distance and had already been struck by her beauty. Pandarus knew this. All he had to do was to arrange for them to meet and to find a way for Troilus to win her heart. But he was old and needed the advice of some young people. I wonder if you can help him?

You can now put the children into same-sex groupings. Ask the boys to come up with ideas for what Troilus should do/say to persuade Cressida to go on a date with him and ask the girls to think of arguments that might persuade Cressida to accept. It would be helpful if you took on the role of Pandarus while they explained their arguments to you. This will allow you to react as pleased, shocked, puzzled, disappointed and so on with their ideas and to question them further.

Make sure to thank them for their interesting and useful advice before ending the activity.

Helen: should she stay or should she go?

> Meanwhile, Troilus, as a prince of Troy, had other things on his mind, apart from Cressida. This very day there was an important debate being held in the palace over whether it was time to end the war by handing Helen back to the Greeks. Hector, in charge of the Trojan army and the city's defences, supported this idea, whereas his brother, Troilus, opposed it. Let's see what each had to say and whom you would support, if you were a citizen of Troy.

Ask for a child to volunteer to be Helen and sit her on a chair at the front of the class with two other children in the role of guards standing behind her. Then tell the class you will take on the role of each brother in turn to deliver their arguments. Do this from opposite sides of Helen, making the following points (the words in quotation marks are text scraps).

Hector: Helen is not a Trojan and does not belong here. Is one life worth the hundreds who have died, 'to guard a thing not ours'? We can't just say she is worth keeping because Paris, our brother, loves her! 'A thing of value must be precious of itself'. She must genuinely be worth the lives of all those who have died and who are still to die. And can we really say this? No, 'She is not worth what she doth cost the keeping'. Beautiful though she is, prize though she is, it is time for her to be handed back to the Greeks, to her true husband. Troilus, you are young and hot-headed. When you are older you will learn how to control your temper and be calm enough to make proper decisions about what is right and wrong.

Troilus: My brother, you are like a man with trembling hands. Is it cold or fear that makes them shake? You can 'fur your gloves with reasons'. But here are your reasons. 'You know a sword employed is perilous and reason flies the object of all harm'. In other words, you want to run away. What you call reason is an excuse for cowardice. You say Helen is 'not worth what she doth cost the keeping' but you agreed with us that the Greeks are far too ambitious and needed teaching a lesson. That is why we all blessed Paris when he returned with Helen 'a pearl whose price hath launched above a thousand ships'. What will it say about our courage – or lack of it – if we now change our minds? 'O theft most base that we have stol'n what we do fear to keep'. Can you imagine how betrayed Paris, our brother, will feel if we now hand Helen back? We made our choice; we must now 'stand firm by honour' and show the courage and determination to stick to our decision.

Now ask the child who played Helen what it was like to have two men talk about her fate like this, as if she were not there. Then invite the children in pairs or small groups to think of some questions to ask Hector and Troilus in turn, limited to five per character. List these on the board or on a flip chart and go back into role to answer each in turn, perhaps recruiting two or three children as advisers to help you find good answers to any difficult questions! Complete this exercise by asking the children to form a line along which they place themselves to show whose arguments they find the most persuasive – Troilus at one end, Hector at the other, with various positions in between according to how strong or uncertain their feelings are. Select a few children to tell you why they have positioned themselves where they have in the line.

Cassandra's warning and Hector's challenge

> Before the meeting was over, however, something frightening happened. Cassandra was the sister of Troilus and Hector. She burst into the room and shouted out a terrible warning. Some thought her mad but some feared that she had the gift to foresee the future. And what a terrible future for Troy she foresaw …

You can now introduce children to the text below and have them work on it using ideas from the section 'Hamlet and the ghost – the choric and the individual' in Chapter 4, page 73.

> Cry, Trojans, cry, practise your eyes with tears!
> Troy must not be, nor goodly Ilium stand –
> Our firebrand brother Paris burns us all.
> Cry, Trojans, cry, a Helen and a woe!
> Cry, cry, Troy burns – or else let Helen go!

Tell the class that, after this outburst, one of the brothers changed his mind. Which one do they think it was and why? Tell them it was Hector who now issued a challenge to Achilles to fight him in front of both armies. Are they surprised? Why do they think he changed his mind? Do they think he was right to do so? In small groups, have the children work on what the words of this challenge might have been and have them call out their different versions from the walls of Troy.

Meanwhile, in the Greek camp …

Play 'Sword and shield' (see Chapter 1, page 17) to capture a sense of tension and threat when crossing from Troy to the Greek camp. Now form the children into a circle and, with your story wand, have them act out the section of the plot below. (The italicised words are text scraps.)

In the Greek camp, things were not going well. All the soldiers were tired and fed up with this long war. The two greatest Greek princes were Agamemnon and Achilles. Agamemnon was the overall leader and proud of it, but everybody said that Achilles was the best soldier of them all. He was strong, he was brave, he was fearless but he was also very big-headed. So when Agamemnon called all the princes together to make plans, Achilles refused to join them. Instead, he stayed in his tent and, with his best friend Patroclus, drank wine, laughed loudly and made fun of the other Greek princes. A messenger brought the Greeks news of Hector's challenge. The princes jumped up and down in excitement. They knew Hector wanted to fight Achilles but Achilles just laughed louder than ever, made rude noises and carried on getting drunk with his friend.

(Use your story wand to clear the circle.)

Now there was another fearless Greek soldier called Ajax. He was big and strong but a bit stupid. If you told him to head-butt a door to show how strong he was, he would probably do it. And his head was so thick he probably wouldn't feel any pain if he did! Well, when he heard of Hector's challenge, he wanted to take it up. 'Me! Me! I'll fight him!!' he kept saying. So the princes, including Ajax, all went to the tent of Achilles. But he wouldn't come out to talk to them and sent out his friend, Patroclus, to tell them all to go away. This made Ajax incredibly angry. He called out '*I hate a proud man as I do hate toads*'. He tried to get into Achilles' tent but all of the other princes dragged him away. This made Ajax more angry still. '*If I go to him with my armed fist I'll pash him o'er the face!*', he called out. '*If he be proud with me I'll freeze his pride. Let me go to him.*' The princes urged him to calm down. 'Are you going to let him insult us? *He should eat swords first!*'. The princes knew they had to flatter Ajax to calm him. 'You are braver than Achilles', said one. 'You are more of a gentleman', said another. 'You are stronger than he', said a third, 'and more intelligent'. This calmed Ajax down. The princes decided to leave Achilles and Ajax agreed to accompany them. He called out one final insult. '*Achilles, you are a dog! I wish you were a Trojan!*'. But Achilles just laughed and he and his friend pulled faces at Ajax as he was led away.

Ask the class what they have now learned about the Greek camp. How would they describe Achilles? Do they think they have met any heroes in the story so far? If so, who and why? If not, why not?

Now play a version of 'Shakespeare sets you free' (Chapter 1, page 15), using a line from the prologue of the play 'Now good, or bad, 'tis but the chance of war'. After the game, ask the children what qualities they have to demonstrate in order to play this game well (such as generosity and quick wittedness). How do these contrast with what they have just seen in the Greek camp?

Troilus 4 Cressida, none truer

While the children are out of the classroom, pin large pieces of paper around your walls with the following text scraps on them.

> None truer than Troilus to Cressida.
> Troilus is as true as truth's simplicity.
> Troilus is as true as steel.
> Troilus is as true as sun today.
> Troilus is as true as earth to th'centre.

Tell the children that these are examples of graffiti that Troilus has been writing on the palace walls and ask what they tell us about his feelings for Cressida. Then tell them that Cressida replied to him, letting him know whether her feelings were as true as his or not. As 'text detectives', can they work with the text below to figure out whether she felt love as truly as he did?

> If I be false or swerve a hair from truth,
> When time is old and hath forgot itself,
> When waterdrops have worn the stones of Troy
> To dusty nothing, when they've said as false
> As fox to lamb, as wolf to heifer's calf,
> Yea, let them say to stick the heart of falsehood,
> As false as Cressid.

A cruel twist

So Troilus and Cressida were in love. Troilus swore that no one's feelings could be truer than his for her; Cressida replied that her love would never be false to him. But this was war and war is cruel. For, unknown to either of them, Cressida's father had asked the Greeks to reward his services to them by making a trade. After all these years he dearly wished to see his daughter again. Couldn't the Greeks, he asked, offer one of their prisoners – an important one – in exchange for Cressida, so that she could come and live in the Greek camp, close to her father? The Greeks and Trojans quickly agreed to this proposal and the very next morning, the morning after Troilus and Cressida had sworn their love for each other, a Greek soldier called Diomedes came to escort Cressida from Troy to the Greek camp. However, when Diomedes first saw Cressida he was immediately struck by her beauty and Troilus noticed this and was very angry with him. But all he had time to do was to give Cressida something to remember him by, so that she would stay true to him, as she had sworn she would – but what could he give her? And what could he say to warn her about Diomedes?

Discuss and note children's ideas about both of these questions, spending particular time over what the gift might have been and what Troilus might have said as he gave it. Then ask for five volunteers to play Troilus, Cressida, Diomedes, Pandarus and a guard and have the rest of the class sculpt them into different images of how they imagine they would have looked as Cressida was being led away to the Greek camp. Encourage different possibilities and ask the children to volunteer words to show what each character might have been thinking or feeling.

Cressida: a woman alone in a hostile camp

> When Cressida was led into the Greek camp she was quickly surrounded by all the Greek soldiers. They teased her cruelly and she looked for her father. But he stayed out of the way, in his tent. There was only Diomedes to protect her. 'Lady', he said, taking her by the hand, 'I'll bring you to your father'.

You can now stage this scene to explore how Cressida might have felt as she entered the Greek camp. Arrange the children into two lines to form a kind of corridor. A volunteer is to take on the role of Cressida. Blindfolded, they are to make their way along this corridor. As she comes close and passes them, children are to 'stab' her with their voices, saying only her name, 'Cressida'. You may like to practise ways of doing this that sound vicious and threatening before running the activity. As she walks down the corridor, Cressida is to stretch out a hand in front of her and is to avoid walking into one of the 'walls'. At the end of the corridor waits Diomedes. When she finally comes close to him he is to take her hand and say the word 'Lady'. At this moment the corridor must fall absolutely silent before he says, gently, 'I'll take you to your father'. This can be played more than once, with different children taking on the role of Cressida, as you gather from the children words that describe what she must have felt like when entering the enemy camp and what it is like to have someone offer to look after her. This might help children understand what happens next.

'O Cressid, O false Cressid!'

Explain to the children that a week later Troilus received a report from a spy he had sent over to keep watch on Cressida in the Greek camp. Tell them you will stage a short scene to show what happened when he received the report (the italicised words are text scraps). Pick up a scroll you have previously prepared and open it. Read it greedily and then look angry/sad and shake your head and mutter, 'He saw Diomedes with it! She must have given it to him! *O Cressid, O false Cressid, false, false, false!*'. Now crumple the letter up and call for your sword and armour. This is the signal for a child you have primed in advance to enter as Pandarus bringing another letter. '*From the Greek camp my lord – it is from Cressida. What says she there?* ...'. Glance at this, tear it up and throw the pieces around the space, saying, '*Words, words, mere words, no matter from the heart*'. (If you don't want to act this scene yourself you can always do it in the form of a story wand activity.)

Discuss what children understand from this scene, then what they think was in each letter. Give them time to discuss possible reasons why Cressida might have betrayed Troilus and what she might have been trying to explain to him in the letter. Versions of both of these letters can be written by the children individually or in groups.

Fair play or fool's play?

In groups of four or five, have the children demonstrate images to illustrate a fair fight and an unfair fight in different modern-day contexts. Discuss what these show and draw from them what the children see as the five key rules for a fair fight. Then give them these lines of dialogue to look at.

Troilus: When many time the captive Grecian falls
            E'en in the fan and wind of your fair sword
            You bid them rise and live.
Hector: Oh, 'tis fair play.
Troilus: Fool's play, by heaven, Hector.

Have children read and comment on their meaning before performing them in their groups with two performing the actions of Hector and a Greek opponent while the others read them aloud. (The action should finish on 'You bid them rise and live' with a strong image that can be held for the final two lines.) The second line is particularly evocative of the swinging of Hector's sword and children will enjoy putting those actions together with the speech. Then explain that this is exactly what happened when Hector fought the Greek champion, Ajax (Ajax, because Achilles had refused to fight him). Do they think this was fair or foolish of Hector? Why?

Achilles and Hector: the two enemies meet

So Hector had fought with Ajax and had spared him, but the two commanders, Hector and Agamemnon, agreed that their armies would meet outside the city in combat the following day. Hector gathered his armour and weapons and was about to return to Troy when he was approached by a soldier who had been watching the fight. It was none other than Achilles, the warrior who had refused his challenge, refused to face him. This was, in fact, the first time the two sworn enemies had ever met. They squared up to each other, face to face, and made a bargain to meet on the field of battle the following day and to fight to the death, each one swearing to kill the other.

Have the children improvise the confrontation in pairs before working in the same pairs on the text below, using the ideas presented in the section 'Breaking the news – working with dialogue' in Chapter 4, page 72.

Achilles: Now, Hector, I have fed mine eyes on thee;
Hector: Is this Achilles?
Achilles: I am Achilles.
              Tell me, you heavens, in which part of his body
              Shall I destroy him? Whether there, or there, or there?
Hector: Henceforth guard thee well;
              For I'll not kill thee there, nor there, nor there;
              I'll kill thee every where, yea, o'er and o'er.
Achilles: To-morrow do I meet thee, fell as death;
Hector: Thy hand upon that match.

'So Ilium fall thou next, come, Troy, sink down'

> Now, do you remember what Troilus called for when he threw away Cressida's letter? Yes, his sword and his armour, because the Trojan army had decided to attack the Greek camp and he was ready for the fight. The battle, when it came, was as vicious as ever, but once more neither army was victorious. Troilus did fight with Diomedes, and we never find out if he kills him or not. However, when Hector and Achilles fought, one of them was slain in what turned out to be a very unfair fight indeed. But which one? And how do you think he was killed?

In groups of four or five, have children discuss which of the warriors they think was killed and how it might have been unfair. Have them explain their reasons before telling them that Achilles' men attacked and killed Hector while he was resting, with no armour to protect him. Then give them the following two lines and let them stage the killing of Hector in their groups.

Hector: I am unarmed: forego this vantage, Greek.
Achilles: Strike, fellows, strike: this is the man I seek!

You might present them with the challenge of making the attack look as unfair and vicious as possible without anyone actually touching anyone else: we have to imagine the weapons doing the work. Our final image should be of Hector, dead and alone. You might also present them with the challenge of making the whole scene no longer than ten seconds in length.

Now choose one of these images of the dead Hector. Ask the children to surround it in a circle and then ask for volunteers to enter the circle to show how Troilus might have reacted on seeing his dead brother. Actively seek out different possibilities here. Choose some that contrast and ask for ideas as to what emotions are on display and what each different Troilus might be thinking. Tell children that the last words Troilus utters in the play are 'Hope of revenge shall hide our inner woe'. What does he mean? Which representation of Troilus best matches these lines in their opinion?

For a very effective conclusion, return to the prophecy of Cassandra 'Cry, Trojans, cry', which the children worked on earlier in the scheme. Have them recall their choric performance of this speech and ask them to perform it again, this time around the dead body of Hector, in much more muted tones. Then, silently, have them encircle Hector's body once more and softly say the line 'So, Ilium fall thou next, come, Troy sink down'. Invite the children to repeat it with you three times in a ritualistic manner. Finally, in a whisper, invite them to fall to the floor, like Hector, as silently as they can. Now bring the class together and ask them to reflect upon what their closing lines would be to finish the story appropriately, if they rather than you were to take on the role of storyteller. And you can spend a good deal of time reflecting upon and discussing the implications of the story with them, what it makes them think about war, about heroes, about the human relationships explored in the play.

Chapter 3

Beginning Shakespeare in the early years

A good early years classroom is rich in learning opportunities that feed children's imaginations. Through a range of carefully planned and structured play, the best practitioners enable and encourage children to create and live in imagined worlds. Role-play, storytelling, small-world play, outdoor play, creating environments, dressing up, making and playing with puppets: all these are essential elements of good early years practice. When they engage in these activities, children bring their particular interpretations and understandings to the process of creating and enacting their own stories.

For many children, their capacity and enthusiasm for playing in these ways begins long before they come to school. They may need little more than a blanket thrown over a table to create a new space that can be imagined as a house, a castle or a cave. As the play grows, more elements are added so that the whole house might be a forest where a scary monster lives – if we hear it coming, we must run and hide in the cave. If they are lucky, young children encounter adults who know how to engage in this kind of play with them, being drawn into their world and believing in it, too. So lunch might become a 'picnic' in the cave, or a parent might playfully take the role of the monster in that joyful scary-but-safe way that young children delight in. And as soon as others are involved, be they adults or other children, the play demands shared understandings and negotiated meanings: we must all agree that the covered table is a cave or the play can't continue.

The parallels with what happens in a theatre are striking. What is used to create imagined worlds may be more elaborate and include sets, lighting, sound and costume. Yet the actors inhabit these worlds in much the way that young children do; behaving *as if* people, places and things are other than they are. Rather like that willing parent, the audience must collude in the pretence: we all know that the actor playing Juliet has not really stabbed herself but we keep quiet, watching and engaging with the story *as if* it were so. It is no accident that we use the word *play* to describe both what happens when a child creates a cave and what happens on the stage; and the subtle relationship between the two offers us rich opportunities to introduce the plays of Shakespeare to children as young as four.

Telling stories

Good early years practice recognises the central importance of story. We read them, tell them, sing them, dance them, act them out with toys and puppets and, through our imaginative play and drama, live them out in action. To do this, we draw on a huge range of sources from contemporary picture story books, to traditional folk and fairy tales, to comic book super-heroes, to film and television. There is no reason why many of Shakespeare's stories should not take their place in this rich mix. *King Lear*, for example, begins with a king who has grown old and wishes to share his kingdom between his three daughters. Before he decides who will have what portion, the king asks which of his daughters loves him most. Wise and foolish kings and their kingdoms are the stuff of stories that have been told to children for centuries; fathers and daughters, sisters and their rivalries are things many of them understand very well from their own experiences. There will be elements of that play and parts of the story which you decide to leave out; Edmund's treachery and the blinding of Gloucester, for example. You have plenty of choices and the stories of the plays can be edited and adapted for young children in many ways. Several authors have written collections of the stories which can be read aloud, the best of which include some of the original language. Some years ago S4C produced the *Animated Tales*, a selection of the plays adapted for children through various forms of animation. Any or all of these might be good places to start but, as we shall see, there are many ways in which we can work more directly from Shakespeare's text to create living stories that children experience through action.

Creating worlds

Much of the action in *A Midsummer Night's Dream* takes place in 'a wood near Athens', although it is clear from the text that Shakespeare had as much in mind the woodland of his native Warwickshire. But this wood is a magical place, inhabited by fairies. In performance, there are countless ways in which the wood has been interpreted and brought to life. Children will happily suggest ways in which they might create a wood of their own. They might use a collection of cloths, camouflage nets, logs and potted plants to create their own version with trees, glades and secret hiding places. In created worlds like these, the teacher can tell and act stories from the plays with children, and they can create and enact stories of their own. Other worlds can be inspired by other plays: what does Lear's kingdom look like? Where do his subjects live and what do they do? Making interpretive choices in response to questions like these and putting those choices into practical action will be very familiar to many early years practitioners; they are just as fundamental to how theatre is made.

Characters and problems

Like any good story, a play must have some sort of disturbance or conflict at its heart. Shakespeare puts his characters through an extraordinary array of experiences and emotions, many of which are more than suitable for young children to explore. But as any early years teacher knows, they are much more likely to do this if these characters are presented to them as living people. One of the best and most accessible ways of doing this is by the teacher taking on one of these parts herself. So, for example, children may have created their 'wood near Athens' and played in it, imagining and enacting the sorts of tricks the fairies might play on the 'mortals' who come into their world. The teacher might then take the role of Puck, calling all the fairies together because he needs their help. In role, the teacher then explains how Oberon, King of Fairies, sent him to make a young Athenian man fall in love with a young woman by putting the juice of a flower on the young man's sleeping eyes. He did as he was told, but put the juice on another man's eyes by mistake and now everyone seems to be in love with the wrong person – can the fairies help him sort it all out? Similarly, a teacher might take on the role of King Lear, telling the children that he wants to give up being king and divide his kingdom. He tells the children about his three daughters, about how Cordelia is his favourite and asks for their advice and ideas for the best and fairest way to share the kingdom out. When we bring characters from the plays to life in this way they become very accessible to young children. If we can also present them as someone who needs help or advice from the children in some way, we encourage children to approach the plays with that sense of purpose and expertise which will be familiar from their other imaginative play and drama.

Playing with language

As we have already discussed, many adults find Shakespeare's language difficult and intimidating, associating it with desk-bound study and analysis of text. When you tell your friends and colleagues that you plan to introduce Shakespeare to young children, you may be greeted with incredulity. But it is worth remembering that young children are encountering and embracing new language all the time. If it is introduced playfully, there is no reason at all why young children should not delight in the sounds and rhythms of the original text. The fairies' song from *A Midsummer Night's Dream* (Act II, Sc. 2), for example, with its spotted snakes with double tongue, newts and blindworms and weaving spiders, is language which young children can readily interpret through song, dance, chant and movement. As long as we approach it in a spirit of playful discovery, much of Shakespeare's language can be just as accessible as traditional stories, songs and nursery rhymes. The importance of children engaging with this language physically and connecting it with the whole body through movement and action cannot be overemphasised: this is fundamental to the approach we take throughout this book.

The plays are so rich in stories, settings, characters and language that, once started, you and your class will find plenty to entice, excite, amuse and enthral. The two detailed examples that follow show how you can build your engagement with the plays into extended learning experiences that reach right across the early years curriculum. What we outline here are a number of activities you can do with your whole class. How long you spend on each will be up to your judgement and the children's responses. Each of the activities we describe will naturally extend into children's independent play and learning so that they inhabit the world of the play as fully as possible.

Example 1 – *The Tempest*

This play begins with a violent storm at sea. When their ship splits, a group of sailors and their passengers believe they will drown. In the play's second scene, we meet Prospero and his daughter Miranda and learn that he has caused the storm through his magic powers. As he explains to his daughter why he has done this, he tells of how he was once Duke of Milan, how he was usurped by his brother, and how he and Miranda came to live on an island. It is with this story that you can begin your exploration of the play.

'Go, stop, show me ...'

Begin by playing this game, described in Chapter 1 page 13, to warm up. Include adjectives like happy, jealous, angry, terrified, excited, all of which are important in the story you are about to tell together. You can also include phrases like 'show me magic powers', 'show me a loving father and his daughter' or 'show me a beautiful island'.

Telling the story of Prospero's lost dukedom

Sit the children in a circle and tell the story using the story wand technique which we explained in Chapter 2, page 21. We have included a version of the story as an appendix which you can use as the basis for your telling. Whether you choose to use this or tell a version of your own, what matters is that the children understand that Prospero was once Duke of Milan, and that he was usurped by his brother, Antonio, who plotted with Alonso, the King of Naples and Prospero's enemy. They also need to understand how Prospero and his very young daughter were set adrift in a boat and eventually landed on an island. As you tell this story, it is important that you include some of the original text (see Appendix). Have these fragments of text printed out on A4 paper so that you can read from them and spread them around on the floor as the story unfolds. They can also be used to revise the story in later sessions, for example with a game of 'Go, stop, show me ...' in which you ask the children to 'show me "the Duke of Milan and a prince of power"' or 'show me "in my false brother awaked an evil nature"'.

Creating the island

There are any number of ways in which the island has been represented in performance, from an arctic wasteland to a tropical paradise, so the children can create their island in any way they like. One of the simplest is to begin with a word carpet, as described in Chapter 1, page 13. You will need plenty of scrap paper (about A5 size), coloured marker pens and a good floor space to work in. Take a few of the pieces of paper to the edge of the room, tell the children that this is where Prospero and Miranda landed, and ask them what it might be like. If they say 'a beach', you might ask them to tell you more about the beach so you perhaps develop the phrase 'a golden, sandy beach with little rippling waves'. Write this phrase on one of the scraps of paper and put it on the floor. Depending on the age and ability of your class, you may want to show them how you can add a picture, or perhaps just draw the beach on the paper. Next move away from the 'beach' towards the middle of the room and ask the children, 'If I walk up the beach and towards the middle of the island, what do I come to next?' They might say 'palm trees' in which case you write/draw these on another scrap of paper and put it on the floor. Once you have given them a couple of examples, put paper and pens around the room and ask the children to add as many ideas as they can by writing and/or drawing and putting their pieces of paper in the right place on their 'island'. This need only take a few minutes before you have created a whole carpet of words and /or pictures across the floor which describe the island on which Prospero and Miranda find themselves.

Exploring the island

In pairs, the children can walk around the island that they have created, talking to each other about what they can see, hear, feel and smell. When you have given them time to do this, bring them together and ask them about the island they have just explored. Ask where their favourite places are, if there might be any dangerous places, or if they found anything surprising. As they answer, extend their responses as much as possible so they begin to use rich, descriptive language to tell you about their island.

The word carpet is a very quick way of creating the island and has the advantage of demanding that children use language imaginatively as they work. You can then use their ideas and language to create the island in other ways, perhaps using cloths, nets and other materials to create an environment in a part of your classroom. They can also make islands with sand and water and in their small-world play. This exploratory play can also extend to any outdoor spaces you have.

Making soundscapes

Read the children these lines from Act III, Scene 2:

The isle is full of noises,
Sounds, and sweet airs, that give delight and hurt not
Sometimes, a thousand twangling instruments
Will hum about mine ears, and sometimes voices
That, if I then had waked after long sleep,
Will make me sleep again.

Ask what sorts of sounds are being described here, then ask them to go and find a place on their word carpet island where they think there might be a sound that 'gives delight and hurts not'. You can have a selection of instruments available, but you may just prefer to use the children's voices. Tell them that when you raise your hand off the floor, you want each of them to start making their sound – the higher your hand gets off the floor, the louder the sounds must get. As you develop and play with this soundscape, have the children perform it while you read the lines again.

Meeting Caliban

Explain that the island is not entirely uninhabited and that Prospero and Miranda encounter a creature called Caliban. In Act I, Scene 2, Prospero describes him as:

A freckled whelp, hag-born, not honoured with a human shape

Read this description to the children and ask if someone can show you what Caliban might have looked like. You can do this individually, but you can also ask children in twos and threes to create a collective image of Caliban. Explain that Caliban is the son of a witch called Sycorax, who died and left him alone on the island. When Prospero and Miranda first meet him, he has no language and can only make rude and disgusting noises. Ask one or more of the children to take on the role of Caliban and another to come and be Miranda. You can take the role of Prospero yourself. Then improvise what happens when Prospero and Miranda first approach Caliban and hear the noises he makes. Explain that they took pity on him, that they 'stroks't' him and gave him 'water with berries in't'. They also taught him 'language'.

'Caliban, Caliban, what can you see?'

Put the children into pairs, one to be Caliban and one to be Miranda. Those playing Caliban show Miranda around the island (which can be your word carpet or any other versions of the island you have created). He points to things, she tells him what they are and then says 'Caliban, Caliban, what can you see?' and he answers. At any point, the teacher can pause the game, point to one of the Calibans and ask the question – this is a good way of sharing as many of the answers as possible as well as keeping the children focused on the game. You can also play the game, asking the Calibans what they can hear, feel and smell.

Prospero makes Caliban his slave

Using the same story wand technique that you used earlier, tell how Caliban and Miranda grew up together and were very happy. Then narrate and act out how Caliban wakes up one night, looks at Miranda and thinks her so beautiful that he leans across to kiss her (the play is rather more explicit than that, but at this age a kiss will be quite enough!). As he does so, Miranda wakes and screams. This in turn wakes her father who is furious and punishes Caliban by racking him with cramps and making him his slave. You can then ask the children what sort of jobs they think Caliban might be made to do. As they suggest the jobs, they must devise a simple mime or action for each and teach it to the rest of the class. When you have about three or four that everyone knows, play the game 'Prospero's coming', described in Chapter 1, page 14. As Prospero, you call out the jobs and the children mime them. But you can also add in 'I'll rack thee with old cramps!' at which all the children must double up as if in terrible pain. When you take the role of Prospero to play this game, wear some sort of cloak and use your story wand to represent your magic staff – these are very important symbols in the story.

'Caliban's footsteps'

Play this game as outlined in Chapter 1, page 16. It is a really good way of getting all the children to remember and speak some of Shakespeare's lines.

Introducing Ariel

Tell the children how there was also a spirit who lived on the island. When Prospero and Miranda first arrived, he had been trapped inside a tree by Sycorax, the witch, and his 'groans did make wolves howl, and penetrate the breasts of ever-angry bears'. But Prospero was able to use his magic to set Ariel free and the spirit had served him ever since. For the purposes of the drama, it is helpful to introduce the idea of Ariel being one of several spirits on the island who serve Prospero: that way all the children can bring their expertise and ideas to the next part of the story. Tell the children that the spirits cannot appear except through Prospero's magic but that they are then able 'to fly, to swim, to dive into the fire, to ride on the curled clouds'. Get them to show you what the spirits look like when they are doing these things. Then ask for ideas about how and where the spirits hide – maybe in trees, or disguised as rocks, perhaps transformed into an animal. Then you can play a quick game. On the command 'Move spirits, move!', they 'fly, swim, dive and ride the curled clouds' around the island; on the command 'Hide spirits, hide!' they must take up their 'hiding shapes' as trees, rocks, etc. and be completely still.

Prospero's servants

Get the children to take up their spirit 'hiding shapes' then, as Prospero with your cloak and staff, call out the lines:

> Come away, servant, come! I am ready now.
> Approach, my Ariel, come!

When you do this, the children move towards you whispering the lines:

> All hail, great master, grave sir, hail. I come
> To answer thy best pleasure. Be 't to fly,
> To swim, to dive into the fire, to ride
> On the curled clouds,

The children may not remember all of these lines but, as we have stressed, if you introduce them playfully and combine them with the 'Move spirits, move!' game, you will be surprised by how much sticks. As the children approach speaking their lines and interpreting them through movement, use your staff to gesture that you want them to sit and be ready to help you.

A spell for a storm

When you first told the story of Prospero and Miranda coming to their island, you probably had children represent Prospero's books simply by holding their arms out so that he could 'turn their pages'. For this next stage you could use that same technique again, or you might have prepared a large book of spells. Whatever you choose, you will need to indicate that, as Prospero, you are finding it very difficult to read what the book says – this is partly why you need their help. Turn to a 'page' and tell the spirits (the children) that this is a spell for making a storm. Ask their help in 'reading' what the spell says – they will quickly pick up on the idea that they need to suggest things that are ingredients for the spell. They might, for example, say 'a crab's claw'. Rather than just accept this as it is, you might say, 'Ah yes, I remember now, but there was something else about the crab's claw – it was a something crab's claw from the something shore'. This will encourage children to make further suggestions, so you may end up with a phrase like 'a speckled crab's claw from the rocky shore'. Then you can ask one of the spirits to go and fetch it for you. Using this technique, you can all devise a spell together. One class we worked with came up with the following:

> Heavy rain drops scooped from the sea
> Glowing pebbles to conjure the clouds
> Sparkling seaweed to capture the lightning
> Huge, heavy rocks to rumble the thunder
> Shell of coconut to sharpen the wind
> Mesmerising sand for the stinging hail

When the spell is complete, mime mixing it all together and pouring the mixture into the sea.

Making the storm

There are many ways that you can do this with the children using sound and movement. You might just use sounds they can make with their voices and bodies – clicking and clapping for raindrops, thumping feet for thunder, etc. – or you might include a range of percussion instruments. It is important, though, that the children control their storm, building it up gradually. You can have them do this by taking the role of Prospero and using your staff to 'conduct' the storm – pointing it to bring different groups of children in, raising it to increase the volume and so on. Not only does this help make a much better storm, it also reinforces the idea of Prospero as the powerful magician who can control the storm very precisely. Once you have modelled how Prospero does this, you can give the staff to one of the children for them to 'conduct' the storm. You will also find it very useful to make a recording of the children's storm that you can use later.

The ship at sea

For this next stage, you will need a piece of cloth large enough for all the children to sit around and hold (dark blue, green or black would be best to suggest a stormy sea). You will also need a simple folded paper boat or ship. Get the children to lift the cloth together and experiment with moving it to represent the movement of the waves. Combine this with the storm sounds that they made earlier, then put the paper ship into the middle of the cloth and explain that they are going to give the ship the roughest ride they can without turning it over. This may be quite tricky to begin with, but controlling the storm very precisely is important in the story. As they watch the paper ship being thrown around by the storm, ask them what they think it would be like to be a sailor or a passenger.

The sailors on the ship

This is where you will find it helpful to have a recording of the storm and you will need to play it as loudly as you can. You will need these lines from the opening scene of the play, printed out and spread around the edges of the space.

> Down with the topmast!
> Yare!
> Lower, lower!

> A plague upon this howling!

> Lay her a-hold, a-hold!

> All lost! To prayers, to prayers! All lost!

> Mercy on us!

> We split, we split, we split!

Read these with the children and ask them what they think might be happening on the ship. Devise actions and movements to go with each line – hauling ropes to lower the topmast, for example, kneeling at prayer, and so on. Then play your recording of the storm and get the children to move around the space as the sailors on the ship, calling out the lines as they go. The louder you can make the storm, the more they will have to use their voices to be heard above it.

The spirits report the storm

Tell the children that Prospero sends the spirits to fly to the ship and watch what happens. As Prospero, use the 'Come away, servant, come!' line to call the spirits to you and ask them to describe what they saw and heard on the ship. How did they hide themselves on the ship? What did they change into?

Miranda watches

Ask the children to sit in a space and imagine that they are Miranda watching the storm from the cliff top. Narrate that she watches the terrible storm and hears the dreadful cries of the sailors. Then she realises that this storm has been brought about by her father's magic.

Allay them!

Set a corner of the room up as Prospero's cave. You might have a small table, perhaps with candles on it, his books, a cauldron and, of course, his cloak and magic staff. Explain to the children that Miranda is going to try to persuade her father to stop the storm. Do this by taking on the role of Prospero and encouraging different children to play Miranda. Ask who would like to be Miranda first and challenge them to remember the lines:

> If by your art, my dearest father, you have
> Put the wild waters in this roar, allay them

This is how Miranda opens her conversation with her father. You and the child playing Miranda then improvise the scene but at any point she can pause and ask for help and advice from the rest of the group, or the role can be offered to another child to continue the discussion. Through this scene you, as Prospero, need to explain that you have done this because the passengers on the ship include your brother, Antonio, who took your dukedom; King Alonso of Naples, who plotted with Antonio; and Alonso's son, Ferdinand. You have brought them all to the island to punish them and teach them a lesson for what they did to you and Miranda.

Tormenting Prospero's enemies

Ask the children what tricks they think the spirits might be able to play on Antonio, Alonso and Ferdinand once they are shipwrecked on the island. Working in twos and threes, get them to make mimes and short scenes that show what they did. You can then watch these as Prospero, thanking and praising them for their skill and ingenuity. Finish by telling them that you want them to bring Antonio to you.

Antonio and Prospero meet

It will be very helpful at this stage if you can get another adult (maybe a teaching assistant) to join you and take the role of Antonio while you play Prospero. The children will keep their roles as spirits, but will be given the job of sorting out the differences between the two brothers. Each of the brothers needs to explain to the spirits what happened, what they did and why. The children will already know much of Prospero's story, but Antonio needs to explain that Prospero left him with all the work of the dukedom to do because he was so busy with his books of magic. In the end, he decided that if was going to have to do all the work of the duke, he might as well be the duke himself! Whenever we have done this with a class, they (as the spirits) have always told Prospero and Antonio that they must settle their differences and both say they are sorry. This happy and tidy ending is actually not so far from what happens in the play. So you can finish the story by narrating that Antonio, Alonso and Prospero became reconciled, that Miranda and Ferdinand met and fell in love, that the ship had not been destroyed by the storm but was 'tight and yare and bravely rigged, as when we first put out to sea' and that they were all able to leave the island and sail home. Ariel was set free and Caliban left to roam his island once more. As he left the island, Prospero broke his staff and gave up his magic.

Necessarily, this version of *The Tempest* takes some liberties with the play and its story to make it suitable for children of this young age. But the essential themes and spirit of the play are there and children get to live out a story and speak memorable lines that will stay with them for the rest of their lives.

Example 2 – The Comedy of Errors

The plot of this play is very complex, but elements of it can be very appealing to young children and give them plenty of scope to invent and act out stories of their own. In the first scene, there is a speech which tells an extraordinary story of two sets of twins, how both sets become separated and how they all come to be in the same city at the same time without anyone realising it. The confusions of identity are baffling for everyone that comes into contact with them, as much as for the twins themselves.

'Go, stop, show me ...'

Begin by playing this game to warm up. Include adjectives like happy, fearful, confused, worried, etc. Then get the children into pairs and ask them to make images of twins, friends, a storm, a shipwreck and a trickster.

Talking about twins

Ask the children if they know any twins. Are there any twins in the class? Are there any in the school? Are any of them identical twins? What sorts of confusion can this cause? Explain that Shakespeare includes twins in several of his plays and that he even had twins of his own.

Playing twins

We have included some games about twins in Chapter 1 – choose whichever of these you think are most appropriate for your class and play them.

Egeon's story

Egeon is a merchant from Syracuse. He is arrested in Ephesus because there is a dispute between the two places and it is forbidden for anyone from Syracuse to come there. Solinus, Duke of Ephesus, tells Egeon:

> ... if any Syracusian born
> Come to the bay of Ephesus, he dies.
> Unless a thousand marks be levied
> To quit the penalty and ransom him.

Egeon has no money, so he faces death. But before the sentence is carried out, Egeon is asked to explain why he has come. The speech which follows is long and complicated but the story it tells is one that young children can readily understand and enjoy. You could easily adapt it to tell through the story wand technique that we used for *The Tempest*, but, as we saw in the last chapter, you can also get children to create images and add lines before they hear the whole story. This can be an effective way of encouraging them to speculate and antici- pate what the story might be, where and how their particular bit will fit in.

Depending on the age and ability of your children, you may choose to make these images one at a time with the whole class, or you may divide them into groups to work more independently. The images can begin as simple tableaux but you can encourage the children to add sound, movement and language so that they create a rich, collaborative telling of the story. You will need images called:

- a happy family
- twins born to a poor woman
- twins for sale
- setting out on a voyage
- a terrible storm is brewing
- abandon ship
- a mother and two children cling for safety
- two ships to the rescue
- a twin looks for his lost brother.

When the groups have made their images, review them as a whole class and begin to talk about the sort of story they might tell. Then tell the children that you are going to give them some lines from the play which they can add to their images in any way they like: they might take one phrase or word and repeat it with them all speaking together, or they might give different parts of the line to different people. We suggest the following text for each image, but you can add from Egeon's speech or take away as much as you think suitable for your class

A happy family

A joyful mother of two goodly sons;
And, which was strange, the one so like the other
As could not be distinguished but by names.

Twins born to a poor woman

That very hour, and in the selfsame inn,
A mean-born woman was deliverèd
Of such a burden male, twins both alike.

Twins for sale

Those, for their parents were exceeding poor,
I bought, and brought up to attend my sons.

Setting out on a voyage

My wife, not meanly proud of two such boys,
Made daily motions for our home return.
Unwilling, I agreed. Alas! Too soon
We came aboard.

A terrible storm is brewing

For what obscurèd light the heavens did grant
Did but convey unto our fearful minds
A doubtful warrant of immediate death.

Abandon ship!

The sailors sought for safety by our boat,
And left the ship, then sinking-ripe, to us.

A mother and two children cling for safety

My wife, more careful for the latter-born,
Had fastened him unto a small spare mast
Such as seafaring men provide for storms.
To him one of the other twins was bound.

Two ships to the rescue!

The seas waxed calm, and we discoverèd
Two ships from far, making amain to us:
Of Corinth that, of Epidaurus this.

A twin looks for his lost brother

My youngest boy, and yet my eldest care,
At eighteen years became inquisitive.

Sit the children in a circle, getting them to perform their images one at a time. As they do this, you can link the narrative together explaining how Egeon and his wife had identical twin boys and how he bought his twins another set of identical twin boys to be their servants. When the whole family sets off on a voyage, they are separated in a shipwreck, the father taking one of the twins and one of the servants, the mother the other twin and his servant. And, as they separate, both sets of twins end up with the same names – the masters both called Antipholus and the servants both called Dromio. When he grows up, Antipholus of Syracuse, who lives with his father, decides to go looking for his missing twin brother. His father follows him, which is how he comes to be in Ephesus. So, Antipholus of Syracuse and his servant Dromio end up in Ephesus where, unknown to them, there is another identical man called Antipholus with an identical servant called Dromio! It is a fabulous confusion, and children will delight in exploring the potential consequences.

A strange town

In the second scene, Antipholus of Syracuse tells what he has heard of the town of Ephesus:

They say this town is full of cozenage,
As nimble jugglers that deceive the eye,
Dark-working sorcerers that change the mind,
Soul-killing witches that deform the body,
Disguisèd cheaters, prating mountebanks,
And many suchlike libertines of sin.
If it prove so, I will be gone the sooner.

Explain that cozenage means a sort of trickery – to cozen someone is to trick them. A mountebank is a hawker of quack medicines who attracts customers with stories, jokes or tricks. Based on this description, what do the children think the town might be like? What tricks get played on people? What would it be like to be a stranger in the town? In pairs or threes, have the children invent tricks that might be played and devise ways of showing them through language and movement. Some of them may know some simple magic tricks already or perhaps have friends and family members who can teach them. Alternatively, they can just imagine tricks and cheats of their own and invent their own ways of showing them. Once they have devised and enacted them, take on the role of a stranger in the town and walk through it, having the children perform their tricks on you as you go. Their ideas for the town and how it feels could also be developed into a word carpet, similar to that used to create the island in *The Tempest*, but focusing more on the confusing sights and sounds of this strange town.

'Tis dinner-time

This incident from early in the play can be acted out with the story wand to give the children an idea of the sort of confusion that arises between the two sets of twins. As you do so, it will be helpful to have matching hats, glasses or something similar to make it clear how the confusions of identity arise. The stages and lines of the story are:

1   Antipholus of Syracuse gives his Dromio some money to look after.

Go bear it to the Centaur, where we host,

And stay there, Dromio, till I come to thee.

2   Dromio of Ephesus comes to fetch his master home for dinner, but meets the wrong Antipholus.

Antipholus of Syracuse:	What now? How chance thou art returned so soon?
Dromio of Ephesus:	Returned so soon? Rather approached too late.
	The capon burns, the pig falls from the spit.
	The clock hath strucken twelve upon the bell;
	My mistress made it one upon my cheek.
	She is so hot because the meat is cold.
	The meat is cold because you come not home.
Antipholus of Syracuse:	Where have you left the money that I gave you?
Dromio of Ephesus:	O—sixpence that I had o' Wednesday last
	To pay the saddler for my mistress' crupper?
	The saddler had it, sir; I kept it not.
Antipholus of Syracuse:	I am not in a sportive humour now.
	Tell me, and dally not: where is the money?

3   Dromio of Ephesus returns home to his mistress Adriana who is the wife of Antipholus of Ephesus. He explains what happened.

Dromio of Ephesus:	When I desired him to come home to dinner,
	He asked me for a thousand marks in gold.
	"'Tis dinner-time," quoth I. "My gold," quoth he.
	"Your meat doth burn," quoth I. "My gold," quoth he.

"Will you come home?" quoth I. "My gold,"
quoth he;
"Where is the thousand marks I gave thee, villain?"
"The pig," quoth I, "is burned." "My gold!" quoth he.

Children can have great fun with the 'quoth I, quoth he' rhythms of Dromio's explanation. You can put them into pairs, one to take the role of Adriana and one Dromio and play with different ways in which Dromio might move to make his explanation clear.

Devising confusions

Now that they know the background to the play and have seen what can happen when masters and servants are confused, the children can work in pairs or groups to devise and share ideas of their own. These can be done as short scenes, or maybe as three or four linked tableaux or mimes.

Brothers and their family reunited

We do not suggest that you go into detail about the play's complicated plot; rather tell the children that the events and confusions are very like the ones they have devised. As well as the two sets of brothers themselves, they leave lots of other people in the town confused and angry. Then ask the children to speculate about how the story might end. How will the two sets of brothers discover the truth about each other? Will they save their father from his sentence? Working in pairs again, give each the lines:

We came into the world brother and brother,
And now let's go hand in hand, not one before another.

Based on these lines, get them to invent mimes in which two lost twins meet and greet each other. You can use some of the hats, glasses and masks from the twins games that you played earlier. Have the children enact their mimes all together, adding some suitable music as they do so.

Telling the whole story through movement

You can now combine the movement pieces you made to tell Egeon's story of the twins' separation, movement from all the confusion and exasperation of mistaken identity and the final paired pieces that show the brothers meeting. You will need to find three suitable pieces of music that fit with the moods the children have created. This final combination will act as a celebration of all that you have learned and made together and the children could also share it with the rest of the school and perhaps their parents before telling them all about the play.

The two examples we have offered here illustrate some of the ways in which children between the ages of four and seven might encounter Shakespeare's plays for the first time. Although we have described these approaches in some detail, you should feel free to make your own choices about what is suitable for your class. What matters most is that these early experiences are joyful and playful, enabling and encouraging the children to approach the plays confidently, with everything they have to bring to the experience: minds, hearts and bodies. In this way we can hope to seed a lifelong delight and fascination with the plays: their stories, characters, settings and language.

Chapter 4

Beginning with Shakespeare's text

Getting to grips with the delights and complexities of his text is fundamental to beginning Shakespeare. Though this can seem quite daunting in the primary years, particularly for teachers who have little experience of the language themselves, there are a range of approaches that can make the language accessible to everyone. Many of us might feel that our own lack of expertise will make it difficult to connect children with language that is over 400 years old, especially if our own first experiences of the plays were not as positive as they might have been. So it is essential that we approach Shakespeare's language with children in a spirit of discovery, in much the same way that a group of actors and their director might in a professional rehearsal room. The process is not so much about right and wrong answers as it is about possibilities, shared understanding and a collective spirit of exploration. If this is going to be engendered in our classrooms, there are a number of principles and considerations that we should bear in mind.

Language, rhythm and the body

As we have already emphasised, this language is best experienced actively, with children up on their feet, moving and doing. Many teachers are now very familiar with the notion of kinaesthetic or bodily learning, but we are talking here about something rather more fundamental than a preference or 'learning style'. This language dates from a time when mind and body were much more connected, when the boundaries between speech, song and dance were much less defined. The beautiful clarity of Shakespeare's words, their remarkable rhythms and poetry, can only be discovered and appreciated if they are experienced with everything that we have: mind, voice and body.

Language and the power of story

We have argued in previous chapters that understanding and engaging with Shakespeare's stories is very rewarding for children at this age, as indeed it is for all of us. Most theatre programmes include a brief synopsis of the plot so that audiences have an overall sense of the narrative of the play. However magnificent the language of something like the Saint Crispin's Day speech in *Henry V* (Act IV, Sc. 3), our appreciation and understanding of it will be so much greater if we know something of the story that has led up to it; of an exhausted army, tired, wet, cold and hungry, and so hopelessly outnumbered that defeat seems inevitable. If we can imagine ourselves as part of that army, then experiencing the language is even more moving. Equally, it would be unkind to explore this remarkable speech with children and not let them know anything about the eventual outcome of the battle. We would certainly not suggest that you should ever study the text of one of the plays in full at this stage; you will always use selected and edited sections. So it is even more important that children understand how the words they are speaking fit into a bigger story, and how their exploration and understanding of the text can deepen and enrich their understanding of the story.

Language and Shakespeare's worlds – real and imagined

The Chorus in *Henry V* invites the audience to join in a collective effort of imagination to bring 'the vasty fields of France' to life on the small stage of a theatre:

> Think when we talk of horses, that you see them
> Printing their proud hoofs i' the receiving earth
> For 'tis your thoughts that now must deck our kings.

(Prologue)

As we saw in Chapter 3, this kind of shared imagining is something at which young children are particularly adept in their own play. Finding ways in which you can support children in doing this together can be enormously helpful in deepening their engagement with the play, its story and its language. This may need little more than, for example, darkening the room and adding some sound effects to create the opening scenes of *Hamlet*. What matters is that we place the language and our shared exploration of it in contexts and settings that are as real as possible for children as they speak the words. Whether the castle at Elsinor, the fields of France or a wood near Athens, a sense of place that we have collaborated to create will make the language vibrant and meaningful.

Some children will enjoy researching the historical details behind some of the plays. *Henry V* deals with events that were real enough and finding out what happened at the battle of Agincourt, or what laying siege to a town like Harfleur involved, will not only reach across the primary curriculum but will also help children connect to the world of the play. There are always ways in which we can help children understand how Shakespeare's worlds are imagined. The 'wood near Athens' in *A Midsummer Night's Dream*, for example, owes rather more to the Warwickshire of Shakespeare's boyhood than it does to anything in Greece. Some very quick internet research will reveal a plethora of ways in which it has been imagined and created on the stage and you and your class can enjoy creating your own version. When you do, though, it is always good to let your design ideas be informed by the language of the play: what will your 'bank where the wild thyme grows' look like? What is so enjoyable and rewarding about working in this way is the virtuous circle it creates, where our exploration of text informs our shared imagining of the play which, in turn, deepens our understanding of the text. The language and the worlds in which it is spoken are inextricably bound together.

The two examples that follow, *Henry V* and *Hamlet*, show what these ideas can look like in action. As you will see, many of the strategies we apply to these plays will be adaptable and applicable to any. As we outline each step, we specify the kind of text and exploration to which it can apply. Bear in mind, however, that none of these approaches is fixed or must be adhered to in any particular way; as you become more confident you will adapt them to suit your particular class and the text you are exploring together.

Example 1 – Henry V

This play is part of what is often referred to as Shakespeare's 'histories cycle'. In the historical sequence of English Kings, Richard II, Henry IV, Henry V, Henry VI and Richard III, it comes in the middle but is the last of the eight that Shakespeare wrote. It has some extraordinarily powerful oratory in its best-known speeches and raises many issues that children can explore: why countries go to war, how the misguided excitement of a foreign campaign can change once the realities become clear, and the devastation that armies can leave in their wake. These are big and complex issues to be tackling with children in their primary years, but the play and its story can help to set up a potent imaginative and reflective process that, if similarly nourished in the future, will mature and deepen as they grow.

The case for war – interrogating text and drawing inferences

When the children first encounter the text in this example, they need quickly to develop a general idea of what the language is about. They can do this in pairs and groups, supporting each other in that spirit of collaborative exploration that we consistently emphasise throughout this book.

In Act I, Scene 3, King Henry has called his court together to advise him about his claim to the French throne. He has only recently inherited the English throne from his father, Henry IV, whose own claim was contested and whose reign was blighted by civil war. As he lay dying, Henry IV advised his son:

> Be it thy course to busy giddy minds
> With foreign quarrels, that action, hence borne out,
> May waste the memory of the former days.
>
> (*Henry IV Part 2*, Act IV, Sc. 2)

In other words, picking a fight overseas is one sure way to unite a divided nation. This short section of text can be printed out along with other extracts from the dukes, earls and bishops who advise the king. Put each on a separate sheet and spread them around on the floor. Each can have a few words of explanation added where needed:

> They would hold up this Salic Law*
> To bar your highness claiming from the female

(*The Salic Law is hundreds of years old and the French say it bars women from inheriting. Henry's claim to the French throne comes through a female line.)

> Go, my dread lord, to your great-grandsire's tomb,
> From whom you claim; invoke his warlike spirit,
> And your great-uncle's, Edward the Black Prince,
> Who on the French ground played a tragedy,
> Making defeat on the full power of France.

(Henry's ancestors have won great victories in France before – he should aim to live up to their example.)

> Your brother kings and monarchs of the earth
> Do all expect that you should rouse yourself
> As did the former lions of your blood.

> Never king of England
> Had nobles richer and more loyal subjects,
> Whose hearts have left their bodies here in England
> And lie pavilioned in the fields of France.
> Let their bodies follow, my dear liege,
> With blood and sword and fire, to win your right.

> In aid whereof, we of the spirituality
> Will raise your highness such a mighty sum
> As never did the clergy at one time
> Bring in to any of your ancestors.

(The Church is offering to raise money to pay for the war.)

In pairs or threes, ask the children to move among the text scraps and talk to each other about what they might mean. Rather than understand them in detail, ask them what particular words stand out and what clues they can find about the meaning of this advice – do they think it is encouraging Henry to go to war or not? At this stage, do not allow them to become too concerned with exact meanings, rather the overall sense of what is there. Ask the pairs and threes to form groups around the pieces of paper which they feel make the strongest case. If some of these groups are too big (more than about four or five), divide them into two smaller groups. The task now is for each group to use the text to prepare a case that they will put before the king. Encourage them to quote directly from the text, but also allow them to use their own words. Explain that you will be organising the space to represent the court, that you will take the role of the king, and that each group will be expected to come before you in turn. Discuss the power that the king has, how he should be addressed and how we will need to behave in his presence. Then give each group time to prepare and practise presenting their case.

In the court of King Henry – improvising around the text

Now children have the opportunity to apply what they have learned from looking at the text to create an improvised scene together. Some will choose to quote directly from it, others to give a general sense of what they read using their own words.

Arrange the children in two parallel lines. Talk to them about how you can create the entrance of the king, perhaps adding a fanfare as he arrives; how members of the court might bow; and how each group will come out in turn to make their case in ways that feel appropriately formal. At one end of the room you can place a chair, which you might cover with a simple cloth to represent the throne, perhaps hanging an English flag over it. You can signal the role of the king by wearing a cloak and crown. Take time to build belief in this part of the story, making sure that all the children take their roles seriously. If at any point you feel they do not, you can show your displeasure through your role as the king, stressing the gravity of the decision that you have to make.

As you have practised, each group will come before you in turn and make their case. After each group has finished, you say the line:

> May I with right and conscience make this claim?

When each group has made its case to the king, talk out of role about what has been said. How do they think the king will react? How strong is the case for going to war with France? Establish a line across the room, perhaps with an English flag at one end to represent 'yes' to going to war, with 'no' at the other end. Ask the children to arrange themselves along the line according to how strong the case is: they do not have to go to one end or the other but can be anywhere along the line to reflect how they feel. Leave asking them what decision they think Henry will make until they have heard what happens next.

The ambassadors of France – performing text in context

The language of the play is now more deliberately woven into the improvised action, heard by most of the children for the first time, and included in a way that moves the story on.

Have prepared a closed box or casket into which you have put some tennis balls. It is very important that no one sees these before the box is opened in the court. Ask for two children to volunteer to play the ambassadors and bring a gift from the Dauphin (the French prince) for the English King. Give them the lines:

> Your highness, lately sending into France,
> Did claim some certain dukedoms.
> You cannot revel into dukedoms there.
> He therefore sends you, meeter for your spirit,
> This tun of treasure.

They can divide these lines between them. If necessary, the scene will work perfectly well if they read what they have to say. Either way, they will need to practise the lines while you organise the rest of the scene. Ask one of the children to take the role of the Duke of Exeter, the king's uncle. Tell him that when the treasure is offered he must step forward and open it. You will ask, 'What treasure, uncle?' He must say exactly what is inside the box followed by the words 'my liege'. Now you can enact the scene, the rest of the children once again taking the role of the king's advisers and courtiers. If it goes to plan, you should be told that the 'treasure', the gift from the Dauphin, is 'Tennis balls, my liege'. From your role as the king, you can challenge the ambassadors as to why they have brought such an insulting gift, but don't leave them struggling for too long! Out of role, talk about how the king might react and how this might affect his decision to go to war. Return to the yes/no line, this time asking the children to stand where they think Henry's mind is – is he ready to lead his country to war?

Preparations for war – speaking text in chorus with actions

This is an opportunity for everyone to speak Shakespeare's language, supported by working in pairs and groups. They will also be helped to make sense of the language by translating it into physical actions.

> Now all the youth of England are on fire,
> And silken dalliance in the wardrobe lies;
> Now thrive the armourers, and honour's thought
> Reigns solely in the breast of every man.
> They sell the pasture now to buy the horse,
> Following the mirror of all Christian kings
> With wingèd heels, as English Mercuries.
> For now sits expectation in the air
> And hides a sword from hilts unto the point
> With crowns imperial, crowns and coronets,
> Promised to Harry and his followers.

The French, advised by good intelligence
Of this most dreadful preparation,
Shake in their fear, and with pale policy
Seek to divert the English purposes.

These edited lines are spoken by the Chorus at the beginning of Act II. There are many ways that you can share this, reading and speaking it together. Begin by reading it aloud yourself and asking the children to listen for any words or phrases that stand out for them. Then read it again, this time asking them to call back and echo those words or phrases: some will be spoken by several children at the same time, others perhaps by just one or two voices.

Now put them into pairs, give each pair a copy of the text, and ask them to share the words or phrases that stand out for them. Each pair then devises an action or movement to accompany their word or phrase and shares it with the rest of the class. They might, for example, choose 'Now thrive the armourers' and mime hammering some armour or a weapon into shape.

The pairs can now come together into fours. Each group can be given a pair of lines from the speech. Because there are an odd number of lines, one group could have the line 'They sell the pasture now to buy the horse' on its own. Their next task is to prepare their lines for performance. Encourage them to read them repeatedly in their groups until they start to stick and they can remember them by heart; combining them with actions will really help. The group can choose to speak them all together or divide the lines between them, but they must add clear actions that bring them to life. When they have done this, you can combine each group's performance to create a unified, active rendition of the speech. Having performed it, they can discuss the mood that the speech creates. Why would people be so enthusiastic, excited even, about going to war? At this point in the work, you may want to show the class some of the recruitment posters that were used at the outbreak of the First World War and talk about how the mood of these and that of the speech compare. It is worth stressing again how much richer that discussion will be because the children have had Shakespeare's language on their tongues and felt it through their bodies.

The siege of Harfleur – one text, many voices

Here children use a number of strategies to explore and understand the text. Doing this repeatedly helps them to become very familiar and comfortable with the language, its sounds and rhythms. This allows them to create a version of a speech which is active, exciting and inclusive of everyone.

You will need to narrate the next part of the story, telling the children how Henry's army crossed the English Channel and laid siege to the French town of Harfleur. As we suggested earlier, some of them will enjoy finding out what the siege of a walled town like this would have involved and just how difficult it would be to attack and breach the walls while under constant attack from the defenders. Urging his army to make one last effort to break through, King Henry utters one of Shakespeare's most famous orations:

> Once more unto the breach, dear friends, once more,
> Or close the wall up with our English dead.
> In peace there's nothing so becomes a man
> As modest stillness and humility,
> But when the blast of war blows in our ears,
> Then imitate the action of the tiger.
> Stiffen the sinews, conjure up the blood,
>
> Now set the teeth and stretch the nostril wide,
> Hold hard the breath, and bend up every spirit
> To his full height. On, on, you noblest English,
> Whose blood is fet from fathers of war-proof,
> Fathers that like so many Alexanders
> Have in these parts from morn till even fought,
> And sheathed their swords for lack of argument.
> Dishonour not your mothers; now attest
> That those whom you called fathers did beget you.
> Be copy now to men of grosser blood,
> And teach them how to war. And you, good yeomen,
> Whose limbs were made in England, show us here
> The mettle of your pasture; let us swear
> That you are worth your breeding – which I doubt not.
>
> I see you stand like greyhounds in the slips,
> Straining upon the start. The game's afoot.
> Follow your spirit, and upon this charge
> Cry, 'God for Harry! England and Saint George!'

(Act III, Sc. 1, edited)

This speech can be developed into a shared performance that captures its spirit and excitement. To begin with, stand the children in a circle and have them read it aloud, passing from one child to the next at every punctuation mark. This helps them attend to the language – and particularly its punctuation – very closely:

Child 1:   Once more unto the breach
Child 2:   dear friends
Child 3:   once more
Child 4:   Or close the wall up with our English dead
Child 5:   In peace there's nothing so becomes a man as modest stillness and humility

And so on. Depending on the ability and confidence of your class, you may want to introduce a 'tap and skip' rule, by which anyone in the circle can simply tap the child next to them on the shoulder and so pass the reading on without having to read themselves. Provided it is not over-used, this can help the flow of the activity. Having read the speech together in this way, talk about the ways in which the lines are connected and flow into one another.

At this point, you can also introduce the children to the iambic pentameter. Explain that it is like the rhythm of the heartbeat: the words 'I am' have the *tee-tum* rhythm of one *iam*. At its simplest, we put five of these (hence *penta*meter) together to get the rhythm. 'Once **more** un**to** the **breach**, dear **friends**, once **more**' is a perfect iambic pentameter. You can reinforce this learning with a game of 'The pentameter canter', as explained in Chapter 1, page 18.

Now you can divide the speech up, giving one line to each child: if you don't have enough lines to go round, either make your own edit of the speech or have two children share a line. Using what they have learned, get them to 'take their line for a walk', moving around the room, practising saying it aloud in different ways until they know it by heart. They will also need to know the line that comes immediately before theirs.

The children are now going to run the length of the room, shouting their line as they go. When they reach the end of the room, they will take up a still image to represent a soldier as he battles to break through the breach in Harfleur's walls. You will need to practise this several times so that one line flows immediately into the next and children run and shout with commitment and energy. You can give the child who opens the speech a flag to carry behind which all the others will assemble. When the last line is spoken, 'Cry, "God for Harry! England and Saint George!"' the whole class can repeat 'God for Harry! England and Saint George!'.

Having created their own performance of the speech, the children will enjoy looking at a couple of film adaptations. The two that are most freely available, Laurence Olivier's 1944 version and Kenneth Branagh's from 1989, give very contrasting interpretations which the children can compare with their own. Whenever we have done this work, children have always agreed that their own interpretation is much more powerful than either!

The night before Agincourt – improvising to prepare for text

You will need to narrate that the taking of Harfleur cost many lives. Leaving some men to hold the town, Henry and the rest of his army set off through Normandy towards Calais, a town which at that time belonged to the English crown. The march is long and difficult, his army tired, hungry and ravaged by disease. The French army catch up with them at Agincourt and the two armies will have to fight. The English are outnumbered by about five to one.

Talk to the children about the mood of Henry's army. How would they be feeling? How has their mood changed since 'all the youth of England were on fire'? In groups of four or five, ask them to create tableaux of the soldiers seated around their camp fires the night before the battle. Talk about how these images reflect the mood, and then ask each group to improvise a few lines between them that give a sense of how they are feeling and what they are thinking. Darken the room, and then tell them that you are going to walk between them, pausing by each. As you stop by a group, their image comes to life and you 'overhear' what they have to say.

Now tell them that the night before battle an unknown English soldier walks through the camp. Use a cloak to signal this role for yourself, and then tell the children that you are going to visit each camp fire in turn and talk to the soldiers. As you go to each group, ask them how they are feeling now, why they joined the army in the first place, and what they think about the king who has led them here. When you have visited each group, take off the cloak and ask who the stranger might have been. If the children haven't already guessed, reveal that it was none other than King Henry himself. Why do they think he did that? What did he hear about himself?

Now give each group these edited lines from Act IV, Scene 1:

> But if the cause be not good, the king himself hath a heavy reckoning to make, when all those legs and arms and heads, chopped off in a battle, shall join together at the latter day, and cry all, "We died at such a place" – some swearing, some crying for a surgeon, some upon their wives left poor behind them, some upon the debts they owe, some upon their children rawly left. I am afeard there are few die well that die in a battle. Now, if these men do not die well, it will be a black matter for the king that led them to it.

Set them the challenge of speaking these lines – they can divide them up and edit them however they like – in a way that echoes and reflects the mood they created as the king toured his camp.

Saint Crispin's Day – exploring oratory

Agincourt was fought on Saint Crispin's day, 25 October. Having heard what his troops have to say about their king and knowing that the odds are against them, Henry must somehow find a way of stirring them into battle. Initially, you can use many of the same approaches with this speech that we suggested for 'Once more unto the breach', but as you and your class will discover, the outcome you work towards will need to be rather different. Once you have explored it together, divide the speech between the same groups that created the camp fire scenes.

> If we are marked to die, we are enough
> To do our country loss; and if to live,
> The fewer men, the greater share of honour.
> God's will, I pray thee wish not one man more.

He which hath no stomach to this fight,
Let him depart. His passport shall be made
And crowns for convoy put into his purse.
We would not die in that man's company
That fears his fellowship to die with us.

This day is called the Feast of Crispian.
He that outlives this day and comes safe home
Will stand a-tiptoe when this day is named
And rouse him at the name of Crispian.

He that shall see this day and live t' old age
Will yearly on the vigil feast his neighbours
And say, "Tomorrow is Saint Crispian".
Then will he strip his sleeve and show his scars
And say, "These wounds I had on Crispin's day".

This story shall the good man teach his son,
And Crispin Crispian shall ne'er go by
From this day to the ending of the world
But we in it shall be rememberèd.

We few, we happy few, we band of brothers.
For he today that sheds his blood with me
Shall be my brother; be he ne'er so vile,
This day shall gentle his condition.

And gentlemen in England now abed
Shall think themselves accursed they were not here,
And hold their manhoods cheap whiles any speaks
That fought with us upon Saint Crispin's day.

(Act IV, Sc. 3, edited)

We have suggested a way of editing and breaking this speech down into seven sections; but you can edit it in any way you wish. Ask each group to devise a way of speaking their lines as they move from their camp fire tableau to one that depicts them ready to go into battle. When they have performed this as a whole class, talk about the impact of the speech and what it is that Henry has done to lift his soldiers' spirits so that they are ready to fight.

Enacting the battle – exploring off-stage action

There are a number of ways in which you might enact the battle. The simplest is probably to get each group to create three or four tableaux and then to devise linking movements between these so that they can join them into a continuous moving piece. You can add to the effect of this by playing music over the action – perhaps something like the *Dies Irae* from Verdi's *Requiem*.

You can develop this further after telling the children something of what happened in the battle, particularly the impact that the English archers had on the French cavalry. Heavily armoured men struggled horribly in the autumn mud as English arrows fell in their thousands. One group we worked with chose to represent the arrows by taping paper streamers to tennis balls and throwing them across the room, above the action. As well as being a clever reference to the Dauphin's gift, the sound the streamers made added to the effect and those enacting the battle fell to the ground as they heard them fly above them.

Numbering the dead – close listening to text

As the music fades, the children can slowly sink to the floor to create an image of the end of the battle. Choose two children to read the numbers of dead from each side. One has a piece of paper listing the French dead:

> Eight thousand and four hundred, of the which
> Five hundred were but yesterday dubbed knights.
> So that in these ten thousand they have lost
> There are but sixteen hundred mercenaries;
> The rest are princes, barons, lords, knights, squires,
> And gentlemen of blood and quality.
> Here was a royal fellowship of death.

Another has a piece of paper detailing the English dead:

> Edward the Duke of York
> The Earl of Suffolk
> Sir Richard Keighley
> Davy Gam Esquire;
> None else of name, and of all other men
> But five-and-twenty.

When they have read these over their image of the end of the battle, talk about what they mean: some 10,000 French dead to only 29 English and, against all the odds, Henry's army has won the day. The children will probably want to do some research to see if Shakespeare's claim is anywhere near correct.

The impact of war – making interpretive choices for performance

Having done all the work that they have, imaging lines, reading together and individually, performing in groups and as a whole class, you can talk to the children about ways in which you might bring this speech to life:

Should not in this best garden of the world,
Our fertile France, put up her lovely visage?
Alas, she hath from France too long been chased,
And all her husbandry doth lie on heaps,
Corrupting in its own fertility.
Her vine, the merry cheerer of the heart,
Unprunèd dies; her hedges even-plashed
Like prisoners wildly overgrown with hair
Put forth disordered twigs; her fallow leas
The even mead—that erst brought sweetly forth
The freckled cowslip, burnet, and green clover—
Wanting the scythe, all uncorrected, rank,
Conceives by idleness, and nothing teems
But hateful docks, rough thistles, kecksies, burs,
Losing both beauty and utility.
As all our vineyards, fallows, meads, and hedges,
Defective in their natures, grow to wildness,
Even so our houses and ourselves and children
Have lost, or do not learn for want of time,
The sciences that should become our country,
But grow like savages—as soldiers will
That nothing do but meditate on blood—
To swearing and stern looks, diffused attire,
And everything that seems unnatural.

(Act V, Sc. 2, edited)

These lines are spoken by the Duke of Burgundy as King Henry comes to the French court after the defeat. Henry has come to woo Katherine, the French king's daughter. There is much to discuss with your class here: how will she feel about this man who has killed so many of her countrymen and is now asking to be her husband? Why might such a match be a good thing for both countries? Can she come to love the young king who will be so celebrated in his own country, or must she just submit and endure the marriage for the sake of peace? There is plenty more for your class to talk about, and plenty more to explore in the text if you choose to, but the activities outlined here will have done much to introduce them to a very remarkable play, the themes of which are as relevant now as they have always been.

Example 2 – *Hamlet*

This play is widely regarded as one of Shakespeare's greatest. As we stressed in the Introduction, the cultural significance of Shakespeare is immense and this play is one of the best-known and most quoted in the entire canon of world literature. Quite apart from that, it is a rattling good story of murder, deception, and revenge – and as if that might not be enough to excite your class, it begins with a group of soldiers who see a ghost. The activities we outline here will introduce children to a play to which they can return over and over again, later in their formal education and throughout their adult lives. In this example, we extend the use of paired and group work and look much more closely at approaches to dialogue.

Lines of succession

Begin by talking about how someone gets to be a king or a queen. How does the throne pass from one to another? Some children may know, for example, that the line of succession in our own monarchy was altered relatively recently when Edward VIII abdicated in favour of his younger brother. Others will know that, to this day, sons have taken precedence over daughters, regardless of age. When they have had the opportunity to discuss this, put the children into groups and ask them to create two tableaux that show how the crown might pass from one monarch to another. Then ask them to add movement and words between the two: it is often helpful to restrict the number of words they can use and ten will be about right in this case. Review the work and talk about what it shows.

Guarding Elsinor – creating atmosphere through text

Tell the children that this play is set in Denmark at a castle called Elsinor. There has recently been a new king. The last king, Old Hamlet, died after being bitten by a serpent while sleeping in his orchard. Although he had a son, also called Hamlet, the crown passed to the king's brother, Claudius, after he married Gertrude, the old king's wife and Prince Hamlet's mother.

Ask the children how many of them have visited a castle. What was it like? Were there places that they found interesting, exciting or scary? Look at some pictures of castles with them and talk about what it might be like to be guarding one at night. Now ask the children to walk around the space. As they do so, ask them to establish a route that they can walk repeatedly, first in one direction then the other, as if they know it really well. Then darken the room and, as all the soldiers walk their watch, narrate the following:

> You are a guard at the castle of Elsinor. You have been a soldier in Denmark's army for many years, fought bravely in many campaigns, and seen many terrible things. Now you are back at the castle in Elsinor and have been put on the night watch. But in all your years of service, nothing has prepared you for what you have seen and heard recently ...

Print out the following text scraps with each line on a separate sheet of paper and arrange them around the room:

Who's there?

Nay, answer me. Stand and unfold yourself.

Stand! Who's there?

What, has this thing appeared again tonight?

Tush, tush, 'twill not appear.

Look where it comes again.

What art thou that usurp'st this time of night,
Stay, speak, speak, I charge thee speak.

Is it not like the King?

Ask the children to walk around and read the lines. Talk briefly about what they might mean, then ask them to choose one or two that they can remember and speak aloud. Now arrange half a dozen percussion instruments around the edge of the room. These will need to be things like shakers, drums and cymbals. As the children resume their roles as guards and walk their route again, you are to move around the edge of the room, pausing every now and again to play one of the instruments. Each time you do this, they are to turn towards the sound and call out one of the lines before resuming their patrol. Once an atmosphere of tension and anticipation has been established, add some more narration. Encourage the children to react and respond as you speak:

As you turn a corner you are met by a terrifying sight. There before you is a ghostly figure in full armour. The visor on his helmet is raised and, though you only saw him a few times while he was alive, the face you can see looks just like that of the dead king. Almost frozen with fear, you try to reach for your sword but, as you do so, the figure fades from view. It will soon be dawn and time for you to end your watch ...

Pause the action and tell the children that they are now going to be the guards of the night watch coming off duty. Indicate a part of the room where they are going to gather, mime removing weapons, cloaks and armour, and be ready to give a report on their watch. As they do this, you enter in role as Barnardo, sentinel of the king's guard and friend of young Hamlet. Ask the other soldiers to tell you what they have seen but create an atmosphere of tension and secrecy by talking only in whispers. Have they all seen what you saw? Why do they think the old king's ghost walks the night? And, knowing what they know, do they think you should tell young Hamlet, the old king's son and your good friend? If they mention anything about the new king and his marriage to the old king's wife, you can say that it is really not our place to comment on such things and that anything we say had better be kept within this room. All this will add to an appropriate sense of tension, fear and mistrust.

Breaking the news – working with dialogue

To prepare them for reading and performing dialogue together, the children need first to absorb themselves in the situation: someone has to tell his best friend that the ghost of his late father has been seen. Once they have done this, the children can approach Shakespeare's lines with confidence and understanding.

Talk to the children about how you might tell someone news of this kind. Hamlet is grieving for his dead father and distressed and confused by his mother's new marriage. Introduce the character of Horatio into the story, Hamlet's great friend, who has been told what has happened by the guards and has seen the ghost for himself. Put the children into pairs and ask them to improvise a scene between Horatio and Hamlet where Horatio tells his friend what has happened. When they have had a chance to do this, ask who is willing to share their work and discuss the similarities and differences. Then introduce the children to this edited scene from Act I, Scene 2:

Horatio:	Hail to your lordship!
Hamlet:	Horatio—or I do forget myself.
Horatio:	The same, my lord, and your poor servant ever.
Hamlet:	But what is your affair in Elsinore?
	We'll teach you to drink deep ere you depart.
Horatio:	My lord, I came to see your father's funeral.
Hamlet:	I pray thee do not mock me, fellow-student:
	I think it was to see my mother's wedding.
Horatio:	Indeed, my lord, it followed hard upon.
Hamlet:	Thrift, thrift, Horatio! The funeral baked meats
	Did coldly furnish forth the marriage tables.
	My father, methinks I see my father.
Horatio:	O where, my lord?
Hamlet:	In my mind's eye, Horatio.
Horatio:	I saw him once; he was a goodly king.
Hamlet:	He was a man, take him for all in all:
	I shall not look upon his like again.
Horatio:	My lord, I think I saw him yesternight.
Hamlet:	Saw who?
Horatio:	My lord, the king your father.
Hamlet:	The king my father?
	For heaven's love let me hear.

Read the lines through together, then ask the children to go back to working in their pairs. Set them the challenge of performing these lines with the same mood and feeling as they had in their improvised pieces, reflecting how Horatio broke the news and the way Hamlet reacted. Ask pairs to perform their work and talk about the differences, stressing that there is no right or wrong way of performing this scene and that theirs is one of many possible interpretations. You can, however, encourage children to find something good to say about each version and to say why a particular aspect was good, hence encouraging critical language albeit framed within positive responses.

Hamlet and the ghost – the choric and the individual

Although the ghost's lines are written to be performed by one actor, like many speeches and soliloquies, they can readily be performed by multiple voices. In this instance, the approach can create an entirely appropriate sense of confusion and disorientation.

Talk to the children about all the ways you could make a ghost appear on the stage. Still working in their pairs, ask them to create tableaux showing Hamlet and the ghost of his father. As you review these, talk about how this might be done on stage. Then introduce this edited scene from Act I, Scene 5:

Ghost:	My hour is almost come
	When I to sulphurous and tormenting flames
	Must render up myself.
Hamlet:	Alas, poor ghost!
Ghost:	I am thy father's spirit,
	Doomed for a certain term to walk the night,
	And for the day confined to fast in fires
	Till the foul crimes done in my days of nature
	Are burnt and purged away. List, Hamlet, O list!
	If thou didst ever thy dear father love—
Hamlet:	Oh heaven!
Ghost:	Revenge his foul and most unnatural murder.
Hamlet:	Murder?
Ghost:	Murder most foul, as in the best it is,
	But this most foul, strange, and unnatural.
	It's given out that, sleeping in mine orchard,
	A serpent stung me, so the whole ear of Denmark
	Is by a forgèd process of my death
	Rankly abused. But know, thou noble youth,
	The serpent that did sting thy father's life
	Now wears his crown.
Hamlet:	O my prophetic soul! My uncle!

Read the scene together, with you reading Hamlet's lines and the whole class taking on the role of the ghost. To begin with, you can use the technique of reading from punctuation mark to punctuation mark that we introduced earlier. But then you can experiment with all sorts of ways in which the ghost's speech can be performed chorally. Perhaps you might choose to give groups different sections of the speech to be delivered from different parts of the room, so that

Hamlet is never sure where the next voice is coming from. You can also experiment with emphasising particular words, perhaps having the whole group echo them. Or you might add sound with percussion: for example one sound, every time the ghost mentions murder, another if he mentions his brother and so on. When the piece is ready to perform, invite one of the children to take your place as Hamlet. When it is finished, ask the child who took the role to tell the rest of the class how it felt and talk together about how Hamlet might react to what he has heard. Knowing what he knows, should he go and kill his uncle right away? Can he be sure the ghost was real and telling the truth?

The gallery of ancestors

Introduce the idea that portraits of Hamlet's forebears hang all around the castle. Ask the children what kind of people they might have been and in what ways they might have been painted. We know, for example, that Hamlet's father was a great soldier, so how might he have been portrayed? What about his grandfather and grandmother? Rather than have children talk about this, get them to show you by creating the poses, if necessary bringing in other children to complete the picture. Once everyone has an idea, arrange the 'pictures' around the room to create a living gallery. Then ask one of the children to take the role of Hamlet as he walks through the corridors of the castle. Get him to pause and look at each picture but, as he does so, they should whisper their advice to him about what he should do next. When he has been to all the pictures, everyone can come out of role, talk about the advice he was given and what they think Hamlet's next move should be.

The play's the thing – interpreting stage directions

Narrate that some travelling players come to Elsinor and that Hamlet has the idea of getting them to perform a play called *The Murder of Gonzago* in front of Claudius and Gertrude. The action of this play is very like the events the ghost described: a man poisons a sleeping king and then woos his queen. Divide the children into groups of five or six and give each a copy of the stage direction from Act III, Scene 2:

> Enter a King and a Queen, very lovingly; the Queen embracing him, and he her. She kneels and makes show of protestation unto him. He takes her up, and declines his head upon her neck: lays him down upon a bank of flowers: she, seeing him asleep, leaves him. Anon comes in a fellow, takes off his crown, kisses it, and pours poison in the King's ears, and exits. The Queen returns, finds the King dead, and makes passionate action. The Poisoner, with some two or three Mutes, comes in again, seeming to lament with her. The dead body is carried away. The Poisoner woos the Queen with gifts: she seems loth and unwilling awhile, but in the end accepts his love.

Tell the children that they are going to work together to turn this into a dumb show; a mimed version of the play which would be performed first. As they bring the stage direction to life, emphasise the need for strong, clear actions and gestures. It is also important to emphasise that symbolic action can be much more effective than naturalism in this kind of work. Take, for example, the dead body being carried away. Left to their own devices, most children will take the body by the arms and drag it across the floor: the effect is more likely to be comic than anything else. Show them how they might put two 'mutes' either side of the body and have them mime lifting it as the child playing the dead king simply stands and leaves the space.

When they are all ready, you can add some music and perform the finished pieces as a sort of movement 'round'. The groups stand around the edge of the space in a 'neutral' position: legs about a shoulder's width apart, arms relaxed and by their sides, head slightly forward. On your signal, one group comes into the space and begins their dumb show. Before they have finished, you signal the next group to start and so on. At points they will all be performing together but at different stages; when they have finished, they return to their 'neutral' stances around the edges of the space. The effect can be striking and, importantly, illustrates how this one stage direction, written some 400 years ago, can be interpreted in a remarkable variety of ways.

'Now might I do it' – exploring soliloquy

The idea of soliloquy – when a character speaks thoughts aloud and often alone on the stage – can be quite a difficult one for children of this age to grasp. Some, however, will be familiar with the idea from film and television and you may well have introduced your class to a similar convention, that of 'thought tracking', in other drama work you have done with them. Like many soliloquies, the example here is of a character trying to decide what to do next.

You will need to narrate that King Claudius is displeased with the play and stops it early. His displeasure at the action convinces Hamlet of his uncle's guilt. Hamlet's mother, Gertrude, now sends for him but on his way to see her, Hamlet comes across his uncle at prayer. Hand out copies of this edited soliloquy from Act III, Scene 3:

> Now might I do it pat, now he is praying,
> And now I'll do 't. (He draws his sword) And so he goes to heaven,
> And so am I revenged. That would be scanned.
> A villain kills my father, and for that
> I, his sole son, do this same villain send
> To heaven.
> O, this is hire and salary, not revenge,
> He took my father grossly, full of bread,
> With all his crimes broad blown, as fresh as May,
> No.

(He sheathes his sword)
Up, sword, and know thou a more horrid hent.
When he is drunk asleep, or in his rage,
At game, a-swearing, or about some act
That has no relish of salvation in't.

When you have looked at and read this text together, ask the children who they think Hamlet might be talking to. They will probably tell you that he isn't talking to anyone, rather he is thinking aloud. Ask them why they think Shakespeare might use this device of having his characters speak thoughts aloud to an audience. How is this done in other kinds of writing, in a novel, for example?

You can then talk with them about what decision Hamlet reaches and why – why does he not kill his father's murderer when he has the chance? The clues are all in the text and the children will surprise you by how much they can work out but it may still be important for you to explain the belief that anyone who dies at prayer will go straight to heaven. Having heard from his ghost, Hamlet knows his father was not so fortunate. In pairs, the children can take turns to perform the soliloquy while their partner represents the praying figure of Claudius.

Hamlet and Gertrude – writing text with creative constraints

Talk to the children about what Hamlet and Gertrude might have to say to each other. What does Hamlet want to know from her? How much does she know about what her new husband has done? Why might she be angry with Hamlet? When you have explored these questions together, the children can work in pairs to improvise the meeting between the two. Review a couple of these improvisations and then set the children the challenge of writing a scene between mother and son, perhaps in iambic pentameters. Rather than making the job harder, this kind of creative constraint can actually free up ideas.

You can then present children with this edited version of the opening exchange from Act III, Scene 4:

Hamlet:	Now, mother, what's the matter?
Queen Gertrude:	Hamlet, thou hast thy father much offended.
Hamlet:	Mother, you have my father much offended.
Queen Gertrude:	Come, come, you answer with an idle tongue.
Hamlet:	Go, go, you question with a wicked tongue.
Queen Gertrude:	Why, how now, Hamlet?
Hamlet:	What's the matter now?
Queen Gertrude:	What wilt thou do? Thou wilt not murder me? Help, help, ho!
Polonius:	(behind the arras) What ho! Help, help, help!
Hamlet:	How now, a rat? Dead for a ducat, dead. (He thrusts his sword through the arras)

Polonius:	O, I am slain!
Queen Gertrude:	(to Hamlet) O me, what hast thou done?
Hamlet:	Nay, I know not: is it the King?
Queen Gertrude:	O, what a rash and bloody deed is this!
Hamlet:	A bloody deed—almost as bad, good mother,
	As kill a king and marry with his brother.
Queen Gertrude:	As kill a king?
Hamlet:	Ay, lady, 'twas my word.

As they read and perform this text together, children will notice a third character in the scene: Polonius. Let them discover this for themselves and become curious about who Polonius is and what he is doing there. You can explain that he is the king and queen's close adviser and has hidden behind the arras (curtain) to listen to the exchange between the queen and her son. Why might he do this? Why does he call out? Who does Hamlet think is there and why does he kill him?

You will now need to tell the children that Polonius has a daughter, Ophelia, whom Hamlet once loved but has rejected after the death of his father. Fearing for his own safety, Claudius decides to send Hamlet to England where he has arranged to have him executed by the English king. After her father's death, Ophelia goes mad and drowns herself. Polonius also had a son, Laertes, who was in France. Hearing of the death of his father, he returns to court, only to be told that his sister is dead, too. On his way to England, Hamlet's ship is attacked by pirates and he escapes and returns to Denmark. Laertes, blaming Hamlet for the deaths of both his father and sister, is determined to have revenge. You can simply relate these events to the children, or you may choose to tell them using any of the active storytelling techniques that we outlined in Chapter 2. In the following chapter, we also suggest a writing exercise to explore a theme based on letters that Hamlet exchanges in order to ensure his escape.

The final scene – bringing text to life in groups

In this last activity, children are presented with the problem of interpreting text so that the meaning and the story that underlies it are made clear to an audience. The demands of this scene are complex but, as long as they approach it in that spirit of collaboration, discovery and creativity that we have stressed throughout, your class should find the challenge enormously rewarding and enjoyable.

Between them, Claudius and Laertes devise a plan to kill Hamlet. Laertes will challenge Hamlet to a friendly fencing match; Claudius will place a bet on Hamlet to win. But Laertes will poison his sword so that, once cut with it, Hamlet will die. Just to be sure, Claudius will present Hamlet with a poisoned pearl which he will drop into his wine. Armed with this information, divide the class into groups of about six and set them the challenge of bringing this edited last scene to life:

A table prepared. Enter Trumpets, Drums, and Officers with cushions; King, Queen, Osric, and all the State with foils, daggers, and stoups of wine borne in; and Laertes.

Laertes:	This is too heavy; let me see another.
Hamlet:	This likes me well. These foils have all a length?
Osric:	Ay, my good lord.
Hamlet:	Come on, sir.
Laertes:	Come, my lord. (They play.)
Hamlet:	One.
Laertes:	No.
Hamlet:	Judgement?
Osric:	A hit, a very palpable hit.
Laertes:	Well, again.
Claudius:	Stay, give me drink. Hamlet, this pearl is thine. Here's to thy health. Give him the cup.
Hamlet:	I'll play this bout first; set it by awhile. Come. (They play.) Another hit. What say you?
Laertes:	A touch, a touch; I do confess't.
Gertrude:	Our son shall win.
Claudius:	Gertrude do not drink.
Gertrude:	I will, my lord; I pray you pardon me. (Drinks.)
Hamlet:	Come for the third, Laertes. You do but dally.
Laertes:	Come on. (They play.)
Osric:	Nothing either way.
Laertes:	Have at you now! (In scuffling they change rapiers and both are wounded.)
Claudius:	Part them. They are incensed. (The Queen falls.)
Osric:	Look to the Queen there, ho!
Gertrude:	The drink, the drink! I am poisoned. (Dies.) (Laertes falls.)
Laertes:	The King, the King's to blame.
Hamlet:	Then, venom, to thy work. (Hurts the King.) Follow my mother. (King dies.)
Laertes:	Exchange forgiveness with me, noble Hamlet. (Dies.)
Hamlet:	O, I die, Horatio! The rest is silence. (Dies.)
Horatio:	Good night, sweet Prince, And flights of angels sing thee to thy rest.

The process of turning this scene into clear action requires close reading of the script, which will need to be done in the spirit of shared discovery that we described earlier. Children will realise, for example, that as Claudius delivers the line 'Hamlet, this pearl is thine', he will need to drop the pearl into the goblet of wine. As each group discovers something, it can be shared with the others until you have a number of clear interpretations and performances of the scene.

One challenge you will need to overcome however, is the sword-fighting. This will need some very careful work from you and the children and there are many ways in which it might be achieved safely. The most effective way we have found begins with the protagonists each having a very tightly rolled sheet of newspaper which they use as their sword: as you explore how this works, the whole class can be put into pairs to try their own ideas out. These 'swords' must be used slowly for the children carefully to work out what their fencing moves are going to be. Once they have a set of moves they can remember exactly, the children can dispense with the newspapers and rehearse them at full speed. As each pair performs, a child can be asked to watch them very carefully while holding two suitable metal objects which can be brought together to make the sounds of the invisible swords clashing – large triangles from the music trolley are ideal. While the fencers mime their action, then, sound effects are being added at points where the swords clash. Done well, the effect can be highly effective: the two metal objects can even be dropped to the floor when the rapiers are changed.

Of course, a great deal of the play has been missed out in the work outlined above: not least some of the most famous soliloquies in the English language! There is, then, much more for you to explore together if you choose to. We do not specify how long you and your class might choose to spend on any of this work or on any one play but, once you have started, the children are likely to clamour for more. How far you take them is up to you.

Chapter 5

How Shakespeare can inspire children's writing

There is an old joke that primary teachers sometimes tell one another. A class of children are on a school outing when a child spots something really interesting. 'Don't tell the teacher,' warns their friend. 'We'll only have to write about it.' It is a humorous reminder that teachers often feel that children have learned something only if it is recorded in some way; and that children find much of the writing they have to do in schools onerous and boring. Most of the work we have been describing so far has been active, vocal and physical, as are the plays of Shakespeare themselves. The language that this work inspires can indeed be harnessed and used to enrich children's writing, but the key to doing this successfully is to ensure that children find the process exciting and enjoyable, not predictable and tedious. You should not anxiously try to ensure that every activity leads directly to some kind of writing. What matters is that, when children do write, it is properly focused and contextualised, thoroughly grounded in the language emanating from the drama work and, above all, engaging and rewarding for them.

Children will enjoy writing a story if it is one they are interested in telling and here your role as storyteller can act as a model for them. After a story wand activity, for example, in which you have used text scraps in the dialogue, children can be invited to write their own versions but only after they have helped you note the key points of the plot and recall the scraps of dialogue you used. They may well enjoy making illustrated versions of the play once you have completed the entire scheme, perhaps as a group or as a whole class in the form of a PowerPoint presentation, to be shared with other classes. Their writing will be most effective, however, when it is a stopping place on their way through the drama, used to record, reflect, anticipate or capture strong feelings. Sometimes, too, it can have a dramatic impact on the unfolding of the plot in the manner that Shakespeare himself uses writing, particularly in the form of letters.

Letter writing in Shakespeare

Shakespeare has his characters write letters for a variety of purposes with varied effects that are always dramatically significant. Goneril writes to Regan to warn her that their father, King Lear, is on his way to stay with her; as a result, Regan and her husband are rudely absent from the castle when he arrives and, to add to the insult, they leave Lear to find his own messenger, the Duke of Kent, in chains. Macbeth writes to his wife, describing not only the witches' prophecy and how the first part of it has already come true, but to inform her that the King will be staying that very night at their castle. We not only see his wife reading his words but, more importantly, we witness their strong impact on her as she begins immediately to plot to ensure that the final part of the prophecy shall also come true. Claudius writes a letter to the King of England asking him to kill Hamlet as soon as he arrives there; in the event, Hamlet substitutes it with a letter of his own and the unfortunate bearers of this are killed in his stead. These letters, then, as well as influencing the action, tell us something about those who write them, or receive them, or both. The first shows us how Goneril and Regan are similarly cold-hearted; the second, that Macbeth appears to be less ruthless than his wife; the third, that Claudius is indeed a villain and that Hamlet, too, can have people cold-bloodedly killed – he just finds it hard to do this with his own hand. What is more, as each is written for a very different purpose, we can imagine how the tone and style of their language must differ: one is a warning to a sister, one a report to a wife, the other a request to a political ally. Two of these letters we never hear and this presents a nice opportunity for children to imagine their content and tone, to attempt to write in the style of the author, always with the specific purpose of the letter clear in their minds. For example, Goneril and Regan are two nasty sisters. What kind of things will Goneril say about her father to Regan? How will she describe his behaviour? Will she be fair or will she exaggerate? What shared memories might she refer to when complaining about her father?

When asking children to write letters as part of the schemes of work in this book, then, it is wise to bear in mind what Shakespeare himself can teach them:

- Letters are written for different purposes – to persuade, to advise, to warn, to console, to mislead, as well as to describe and report on action. All of these require careful and different uses of language.
- Letters are written with specific audiences in mind and how people respond to what they read in them can be very significant.
- Letters can be substituted, fall into the wrong hands, bear false witness, persuade people to do something foolish – in other words, their effects can be gripping, tragic, revelatory or just very mischievous!

Because letters play an important part in Shakespeare's plays, we begin this chapter with special attention to them before moving on to explore other forms of writing. Our focus is initially on schemes already described, before outlining a new example intended to illustrate how writing can become a central part of a scheme of work whilst still re-enforcing the active physical and oral approaches that should always be at its core. Although the examples are focused on individual schemes, they are intended to be readily transferable to work on a variety of his plays.

Letters that report on action: examples from *Henry V*

Not until the First World War were the majority of common soldiers literate. Their voices are largely absent from accounts of warfare before that time but since then a series of publications of personal journals and letters have presented vivid accounts of what life could be like for the ordinary soldier at war. Letters to loved ones at home are often particularly evocative. Of course, these were written for different purposes – perhaps to reassure them that all was well; perhaps to reveal the awful truth of war in the face of lies and propaganda; perhaps to convey a vivid and memorable experience, so that the reader could feel a part of it. All of these are possible motives for the children to write in the voice of common soldiers in the scheme of *Henry V*, outlined in the last chapter.

To begin with, after working on the speech 'Now all the youth of England are on fire', they could attempt to convey the atmosphere of excitement and optimism in the port of Southampton as the troops are about to embark. After the siege of Harfleur, they could be asked to write a letter reporting on what the King had said to urge on his troops and the effect his words had had on them and their fellow soldiers. On the night before Agincourt, children could be asked to describe how they felt as individual soldiers, knowing that this could be their last ever communication with their families. What would be the tone of such a letter, reporting on the kind of conversations going on around the campfires? For their fourth and final letter, children could write of the relief and jubilation that they felt on the night after the battle of Agincourt and of their shock on learning the extent of the losses suffered by each side. You could, perhaps, divide the class in two and have half the children write home in the voice of a triumphant English soldier and the other as a defeated and fleeing French soldier, who knows that Henry has ordered that all French prisoners are to be killed. How will each describe the same events differently? Can both sets of letters nonetheless convey some sense of the horrific slaughter and the effect this has had on individual soldiers?

For this, and for any other writing associated with work on the plays, it is important for you to capture the language when it is at its most intense, immediately in and around the drama work. It will help greatly if children have a writer's notebook to hand at all times, which can be used for writing in role, capturing the words, sounds and images they have just witnessed in their own and their classmates' work. Sometimes you might want to record the language together, on flip-chart paper or as a word carpet, on which children are asked, for example, to imagine things they might see, hear, smell or feel inside as they walk around immediately after the battle of Agincourt. Or perhaps you might create a soundscape of the battle, using instruments and words and asking children to help you list the various sounds they could hear during the battle itself. Whatever you do during drama time, whether in your classroom or in some other space, these ways of capturing the language close to the moment of experiencing it are crucial. Only then will it become a resource for English or literacy lessons capable of adding richness, power and beauty to the quality of children's formal writing.

Each time children complete one of the four different letters, you might choose one or two to explore the possible effects on those who read them, as Shakespeare does himself. A good way to do this is to sit the children in a circle, take on the role of the mother or father of the soldier, read the letter out loud with no emotion and then ask the children if that was the way they think it would have been read. At what points in the reading might the parent have shown excitement, relief, sorrow, anxiety? How might they do this with their body language and in their tone of voice? Can any child demonstrate for you so that you get it right when you read it a second time?

Examples of writing opportunities from other schemes in this book

The approach to letter writing outlined above is readily transferable to work on other plays. So, for example, one of the guards on watch at Elsinore might write home in an attempt to convey the fear he and his fellows felt on the appearance of the ghost. Or after the work on Hamlet's meeting with Horatio, where he learns of the ghost's appearance, children might be asked to imagine that Horatio actually informed Hamlet via a letter and that Hamlet wrote a reply to him – what would these letters have said? In both cases, it is paramount that children systematically harness and make use of the language they encounter in the drama work if their writing is properly to benefit from it.

Hamlet also provides us with a very good example of how Shakespeare uses letters to change the action as well as to report on it. On board the ship to England, Hamlet manages to steal the letter written by Claudius ordering his execution and switches it with another demanding that the bearers of the letter, rather than the prince, be summarily executed. Once again, as it is the *effect* of these letters that matters, we never hear their actual words, just a summary of their content. This, then, gives children the chance to imagine what was actually written in them and there are various ways in which you might approach this task. One way might be for you to write a version of the original letter from Claudius yourself, in your best handwriting, and to offer this to the class to study the style of the language, so that Hamlet's forged letter will be convincing. There is also the added challenge of attempting to write in the king's own hand – hence setting a handwriting task with an enjoyably mischievous purpose rather than merely a technical focus. Children will also enjoy attempting to make the letter look as authentic as possible – what will the paper look like? How will it be sealed? Perhaps the head teacher might even be invited to judge the best forgery and provide a suitable reward!

In the scheme of *Troilus and Cressida*, we have two equally intriguing letters for the children to attempt, namely the one written by Troilus's spy in the Greek camp and that written by Cressida, which Troilus reads and rips up, discarding it as 'mere words, no matter from the heart'. Both should differ in tone and intention, even though they deal with the same events, which children in this case are to imagine for themselves. Here you might have children work in pairs, trying to produce a letter each, the one ironically contrasting with the other.

Letters, then, provide a particularly rich and productive vein of language possibilities for you to mine as part of your teaching of Shakespeare. But there are, of course, other opportunities for writing, equally challenging and enjoyable. In *Troilus and Cressida*, for example, we have Hector's challenge to Achilles, to be shouted from the walls of Troy. In *The Winter's Tale*, we have the papers disclosing Perdita's true identity and found in the box by the shepherd – another occasion when children will enjoy making the documents (and the box!) look as authentic as possible. It would be perverse, indeed, to be working with Shakespeare and not to seize suitable opportunities for children to write dialogue. We have presented a model of how to do this in Chapter 4, in the scene between Hamlet and Horatio and in more detail when Hamlet meets with Gertrude. Shakespeare is also famous for his soliloquies, where characters present the audience with their innermost thoughts. A good way to prepare for writing of this kind is for children to write something that would go into a personal journal, not meant for the eyes of anyone else, where a character might express their emotional upheavals – doubts, worries, anguish, pain, excitement, anger, dreams of revenge and so on. This can provide a bridge into soliloquy, as we illustrate in the next section in a scheme based on *Twelfth Night*.

The work for the early years described in Chapter 3 also provides numerous opportunities for young children to write at an appropriate level, perhaps co-operatively with the teacher. 'Writing' the island where Prospero and Miranda are washed ashore through creating a word carpet is one such example. Later, when children have helped to invent the spell that will conjure up the storm, they can write it with suitable illustrations. Perhaps they could be asked to speculate what Caliban might have written in a letter to Miranda to apologise for frightening her; or to write short, illustrated extracts from Miranda's journal at different points in the story. Small groups of children will certainly enjoy creating slides for a shared PowerPoint presentation of their version of *The Tempest* once you have completed the scheme. *The Comedy of Errors* offers other possibilities for written work, particularly with regard to the missing childhoods of the two identical twin brothers, Antipholus of Ephesus and Antipholus of Syracuse. How might these have been different? Children could create two photograph albums, one for each brother, with captions underneath each photo, beginning with the shipwreck. With each of these plays, as with the previous examples in this chapter, it is the strong contexts that the stories present that will motivate children to write.

Example: the story of Malvolio from *Twelfth Night*

The story of Malvolio is a subplot in one of our favourite Shakespeare comedies, *Twelfth Night*. He is the stern, puritanical steward to the beautiful duchess, Olivia, who falls foul of a gang of drunken revellers that includes Olivia's uncle, Sir Toby Belch; Maria, her wily lady in waiting; the idiotic Sir Andrew Aguecheek; and an enigmatic clown called Feste. In their plot for vengeance, the gang play upon Malvolio's vanity and his secret attraction to Olivia by forging a letter in her handwriting and leaving it for him to find in the garden. The letter intimates that she will find him irresistible if he wears some specific, ridiculous clothing and comports himself in a particularly clownish manner. (This letter, incidentally, contains one of Shakespeare's most famous lines: 'Some are born great, some achieve greatness, and some have greatness thrust upon 'em.') Malvolio is completely taken in and utterly delighted, dressing and walking accordingly as he accosts Olivia in the garden to great comic effect. In subsequent scenes, however, the prank turns very dark. Sir Toby's cronies kidnap and imprison Malvolio in a darkened room, tormenting him in an attempt to convince him that he has gone mad. When he is eventually released, he approaches Olivia to protest, still completely baffled by what has happened. On hearing about the joke he exits with a grandiose and prophetic threat: 'I'll be reveng'd on the whole pack of you!'.

As so often with Shakespeare, the story contains character types that children know all about – people who stop them making a noise and having fun, practical jokers and bullies, people who are easily teased and deceived. Spoiling, teasing, ganging up on someone, deceiving, getting your own back, going too far with a joke – all of these themes can be readily explored through this tale. The great appeal for the playful teacher is that it can be done comically and not sanctimoniously, another example of how, when using Shakespeare, you and your class can have your cake *and* eat it!

The scheme that follows can be readily adapted for either upper or lower juniors. Depending on the age and ability of your class, you can edit the language, adapting it and the activities themselves so that the children can readily engage with them.

Introducing the story

Begin by asking the children about times when someone has upset them and their friends by spoiling their fun; and about times when they have played some kind of joke on someone, perhaps as a form of revenge. Then inform them that this is at the heart of the drama work you will do together, taken from one of Shakespeare's very best comedies. Introduce them to the characters by playing 'Go, stop, show me'. 'Show me a beautiful duchess – she is called Olivia'; 'Show me a drunken uncle – he is called Sir Toby Belch'. Other characters include: an upper-class twit (Sir Andrew Aguecheek); a pretty but cunning serving maid (Maria); a clever clown (Feste); and a strict and serious head servant (Malvolio).

You can now explore the actual story with the children, perhaps by acting it out with the story wand or by making key images with selected text, as we described in the scheme for *The Winter's Tale* in Chapter 2. If you choose the latter, then the possible key scenes/lines are listed below. When you insert the narrative links, make sure that these help children to make sense of the characters and the plot – the anger of the partygoers; the fact that Malvolio might persuade Olivia to send her uncle away; the fact that Malvolio is tricked into dressing and acting foolishly, etc. You may also need to provide time for discussion to ensure that children understand the logic of the story.

A wild and noisy party

Sir Toby: Shall we rouse the night-owl?
Maria: What a caterwauling do you keep here!

Malvolio breaks up the party

Malvolio: My masters, are you mad? Is there no respect of place, persons or time
             in you?

A plan of revenge is hatched

Maria: I can write very like my lady your niece.
Sir Toby: He shall think by the letters that thou wilt drop that she's in love
             with him.

A false letter is planted and Malvolio is tricked

Malvolio: I do not now fool myself, for every reason excites to this, that my
             lady loves me.

The gang hides and watches someone make a fool of himself

Malvolio: Sweet lady, ho, ho.
Olivia: Why, this is very midsummer madness!

Tied up, blindfolded and tormented

Malvolio: I am not mad, sir Topas. I say to you the house is dark.
Clown: Madman, I say there is no darkness.

Malvolio learns the truth

Olivia: Malvolio, this is not my writing. 'Tis Maria's hand.

Malvolio swears his revenge

Malvolio: I'll be reveng'd on the whole pack of you!

What was in the forged letter?

Draw children's attention to what we know and what we don't know about the
forged letter at the heart of this prank. In the version above, the only clue to the
trick is that the letter made Malvolio think that Olivia was in love with him. (You
could, if you wish, even remove this clue.) There is much for the children to
think about in order to decide, if they were helping Maria write the letter, how
exactly they would want Malvolio to act in order to look like a complete fool in
front of the lady who is effectively his boss. You could now take on the role of
Maria as you ask children for their advice, discussing and noting down the best

ideas with phrases like 'Oh, yes, Lady Olivia hates men who dress/smell/walk/ look like that!'. As with the letter from Claudius earlier, we need to persuade Malvolio that it is indeed written in Olivia's hand and, with older children, in her style of language. For this you could take some lines that she speaks in the play and write them in your best handwriting, framing them in the form of a letter, for children to imitate as best they can when they write their own versions of Maria's letter. The following lines are taken from Act III, Scene 4:

> Dear friend
> Here, wear this jewel for me, 'tis my picture:
> Refuse it not, it hath no tongue to vex you:
> And I beseech you come again tomorrow.

With older children you might add the following lines from Act III, Scene1, which could provide them with some interesting ideas to include in Maria's letter:

> O world, how apt the poor are to be proud!
> If one should be a prey, how much the better
> To fall before the lion than the wolf.

Again with older children, once they have written their own versions, you might present them with an edited version of the actual letter from the play, keeping in the details of how Maria suggests that Malvolio should dress and smile. You can explore the text with children standing in a circle, reading from punctuation mark to punctuation mark, and selecting key words to physicalise what they particularly like.

What happened in the garden?

In groups of four or five, children can now use ideas from their letters to improvise short plays that show how Malvolio followed Maria's suggestions when he accosted Olivia in the garden. These will also include some dialogue between the gang members, hiding and watching their plan unfold. Once children have shared these with their classmates, they can be asked to compose letters that they imagine Sir Toby Belch might have written to a friend of his, describing their plot, celebrating its success and giving vent to his own feelings of great satisfaction. Before they do this, make sure that you help them to capture the language in ways suggested in the first half of this chapter. Older children can be given the challenge of making him sound unpleasant as he revels in Malvolio's foolishness and can discuss how they might achieve this.

'Never was man thus wronged!'

Present children with the following words uttered by Malvolio, in which he describes to Feste, the clown, how he is being tormented, not knowing that Feste is, in fact, his chief tormentor: 'They have here propertied me: keep me in

darkness, send ministers to me, and do all they can to face me out of my wits.'
Discuss what this tells us and then have the children enact Malvolio's ordeal.
First of all, share out the following phrases, explaining that they are spoken to
Malvolio by members of Toby's gang:

> Malvolio the lunatic;
> Fie, thou dishonest Satan;
> Madman, thou errest;
> There is no darkness but ignorance;
> Fare thee well;
> Remainst thou still in darkness.

Make sure that each child understands and can say their phrase fluently and have
them experiment with ways of making it sound frightening (a loud, hoarse whisper is often scarier than a scream or shout). Then encourage children to try
making unnerving sound effects with their voices – evil-sounding laughter, loud
sighing and so forth – before organising them into two lines and leading a volunteer as Malvolio, blindfolded, between them. Afterwards, ask the child how
Malvolio must have felt.

A more daring and possibly more effective way of playing this is to have the
children stand in a circle with Malvolio sitting on a chair in the middle. Children
then approach him from different directions, perhaps whispering loudly in his ear,
perhaps sneering and laughing as they say their phrase in front of him. Each time
this happens, the child as Malvolio is to say, pleadingly, 'Good sir Topas, do not
think I am mad!'. Every now and then laughter, sighing, distant screaming or
other spooky sounds are made by those in the circle. You need to ask for a volunteer to be Malvolio and make it clear that you need a child with strong nerves!

Whichever way you choose to play this scene, it is well to follow it with a version of the game 'We do but keep the peace'. Repeat the previous exercise but
this time Malvolio wears no blindfold and is to sit on his chair and try to remain
smiling throughout. Each time someone approaches him he is to look at them
calmly and reply with his line, in as calm a voice as possible: 'Good sir Topas, do
not think I am mad'. You can discuss the contrasting ways it felt for Malvolio and
his tormentors in the two exercises and ask children if there is anything to learn
from this about how to face up to name-calling and verbal bullying of this kind.
If you have two children playing Malvolio at the same time, the game has a very
different dynamic and this, too, you can discuss within the context of bullying.

A soliloquy for Malvolio

Children can now be invited to reflect upon Malvolio's thoughts and feelings
while he is sitting, tied up and alone in a darkened room. You need to pose some
focused questions to help them track how these might develop, noting down
good words and ideas that the class comes up with.

So what did we learn about how Malvolio was feeling while he was being tormented in that way? Can we use some of these words to make sentences to show how frightened and confused he felt? Perhaps he then begins to think about who might have brought him here and why. Will he understand why people might think he was mad? How might he want to convince them that they are wrong? Perhaps then he would start to feel angry with his unknown tormentors and think about different things he would like to do to them when he gets out!

Children can then be asked to write their own rough versions of Malvolio's inner monologue in the form of a journal entry before working in ability groups at creating a soliloquy together. In this case, children could be given the additional challenge of trying to write in iambic pentameters. Those children who find writing more difficult often enjoy this constraint as it adds a playful dimension to the writing process. When complete, each group could be asked to perform their soliloquy as a chorus, using ideas for this kind of work outlined in Chapter 4.

'I'll be reveng'd on the whole pack of you!'

To complete the scheme, children could be asked to imagine what plan Malvolio might have come up with to get his revenge on Sir Toby and his cronies. They could work in small groups to act out their ideas, before scripting them in the form of a short playlet. For older children, you can ask for this playlet to be sufficiently clear and coherent for another group to rehearse and perform. The scripts will then be passed on and every group will need to interpret and perform another group's ideas.

Chapter 6

Shakespeare, performance and the primary school

Most teachers who work in primary schools will appreciate the value of children's performances. Whether it is the Christmas play, a summer concert or just a class performing an assembly to which they invite their parents, the best have the power to draw everyone associated with the school into joyful, shared experiences that celebrate what has been achieved and help to build a strong sense of community. Many of us will also recognise that these events can be very stressful as we live in dread of forgotten lines, missed entrances, slipping costumes and collapsing sets. A quick look at some of the more unkind videos uploaded to the internet will illustrate that things may not always go to plan! So the prospect of children as young as four performing something so complex and challenging as Shakespeare in front of their friends and family may be daunting. In this chapter we will show how high-quality ensemble performance can grow readily out of children's engagement with, and exploration of, the plays.

Throughout we have emphasised the need for active approaches to the plays. What we have outlined in previous chapters owes much to the ways in which many actors approach the text in a professional rehearsal room. We have stressed that this language was written to be performed and is best understood through action. So much of what we have described is essentially about collective making: working together to bring stories to life; putting dialogue into action; or creating a whole-group version of a speech like 'Now all the youth of England are on fire'. When we do these activities in the hall or the classroom, we are already, in effect, creating a performance. And when, for example, a class divides into groups to create images that tell the story of *The Winter's Tale*, they will generally clamour, 'Can we show ours?'. That sharing with the rest of the class is a performance and, as they grow and refine their work, they will soon be asking if they can show it more widely – to another teacher, another class, perhaps to the whole school in an assembly. From there to creating an exciting, engaging and moving performance that can be shared with parents and community is a step that you or any class can take, provided you remember some essential principles.

Working as an ensemble

In the best primary classrooms the spirit of ensemble already exists. In many schools, children stay together through most of their primary years and good teachers work hard to encourage a feeling of togetherness, of shared endeavour and purpose, and of valuing and celebrating everyone's contribution to a greater whole. Essentially, that is the principle of ensemble to which many theatre companies also aspire: working and learning together to create something which depends on the efforts of all yet is so much greater than any one individual.

In Chapter 1 we included a section on games that help to build this sense of ensemble. Of course, they cannot do that on their own and they often serve to celebrate such a spirit as much as they do to create it. Many teachers will recognise that a very simple game like 'Go/stop together' can be challenging enough for some classes and the individuals within them. But the more we play and persevere together, the better we get. That spirit is taken into the ways in which we explore the plays together when we accept that none of us – including the teacher – has all the answers. When we carry the principle of ensemble into performance, each child understands that their contribution is essential for the whole to work but that no individual is any more important than another. If I play my part well and trust others to do the same, our performance can only be a success.

The teacher as director

We will all be familiar with the image of the frustrated teacher who, with only a day or two to go to the first performance, is shouting at a group of children and wondering if they will ever get it right – many of us because we have done so ourselves at some time! It is very tempting to think that our role as director should be to tell children where to stand, what to say and how to say it clearly enough for everyone to hear. This is generally a recipe for unnatural and wooden performances, and if we try to take such an approach with language as complex as Shakespeare's we are most unlikely to succeed. Effective directors observe, reflect back on what they can see and hear and ask the right questions to steer and guide to the next stage – just like the best teachers do. If you see your role in this way – as facilitator, questioner, challenger and enabler – you are far more likely to develop a performance that is a genuine collaboration, one that the children recognise as *their* work and *their* responsibility.

Language and the body

Have you ever wondered why we talk about knowing a speech *by heart*? It reflects the way in which language – be it poetry, lines from a play or the words of a song – come to mind in an effortless, rhythmic and pleasurable way. This happens most when it is stored deep within us and has strong associations. Actors will often talk about the lines from a play being 'in the body', reflecting how they associate language with actions, reactions and feelings. Many will tell you how the language 'sticks' through the rehearsal process and exactly the same can happen for children. Take, for example, the approach we took to 'Once more unto the breach' in Chapter 4: we know that many children who have taken part in such an activity will leave knowing most or all of the speech because they associate it with how they moved and felt as they were performing it. It is important to trust this principle when developing work for performance with children so that they feel confident in their ability to remember lines through performing them with commitment, energy and belief. It can be very helpful to have someone hear children talk through their lines but this is likely to come at a later stage, when they already know most of them through the active rehearsal process.

A sense of audience

Although many of the approaches that we have outlined lead to outcomes that we share with each other, the results are likely to need more work before they can be put before an audience. How will our intentions and understandings be made clear to those who are seeing a performance for the first time? How will we make sure our audience can see and hear enough to make sense of what is happening? These are questions that you and your class need to explore and answer together. To do that, they need to know they are part of the rehearsal process at all times. If some children are not directly involved in a scene, encourage them to form the audience and attend carefully to what is being done, drawing observations and comments about what works well, what could be improved and how.

Stages and spaces

Some primary schools have inherited a traditional, raised stage in the form of a proscenium arch at one end of the hall. In our experience this is rarely the best space from which children can share their work. Projecting from there to the back of a school hall demands technical skills that would stretch many trained actors and it is unlikely to show the kind of dynamic, three-dimensional work you have devised together to its best effect. So it is worth thinking about other arrangements. Performing in the round is certainly an option but one of the best can be to perform in the thrust, with the audience seated on three sides. If you are going to do this, it is important to introduce it as early as possible, always encouraging the children to think how their work will sound and look from different parts of the audience and refining it accordingly. Not only will you need to get children to view the work from all the different places in which the audience will sit, you will need to do the same yourself.

The story always wins

We have used this idea, articulated by author Philip Pullman, elsewhere in the book. In the primary school you are always going to perform edited versions of the plays, focusing on key scenes and speeches. Bearing in mind that the majority of your audience will be much less familiar with the play than you and the children, how will you make it clear to your audience that the pieces you have chosen connect into an overall narrative? Some performances make use of a single narrator who reads links between each piece and this can certainly be effective, particularly if the children have written these themselves. As we saw in Chapter 2, though, there are many more possibilities for telling a story in active collaboration. One of the best examples of this in professional theatre can be seen in the Royal Shakespeare Company production of *Nicholas Nickleby* (widely available on DVD) where an ensemble of actors tells the story together through words and actions. Look at the way they update an audience with 'the story so far' and you will see that it is remarkably similar to the story stick or 'whoosh' techniques we described in Chapter 2. However you choose to do it, it is important that the energy of the narrative is maintained and the story keeps driving forward.

The power of symbol

As we saw in Chapter 3, very young children are comfortable using objects symbolically in their play: a cloth over a table can be Prospero's cave; a piece of rope a deadly snake. Live theatre makes much greater use of this kind of symbolic representation than film or television. If someone is stabbed on film, we expect to see plenty of realistic blood; on the stage a strip of bright red cloth will often do the job far more effectively. This is a very important principle to explore with children and one of the best ways is through the 'Show me a ...' game that we described in Chapter 1. Put children into groups and ask them to 'Show me a sailing ship' and you will get a range of creative representations. Give each group a couple of pieces of cloth and perhaps a length of rope and you will soon have all sorts of possibilities that are truly inventive and can be visually exciting on stage. Most children have much more experience of film and television than they do of live theatre so this capacity for symbolic representation may need to be rediscovered and, of course, we do that best through playing together.

You can apply this same principle to costume. It is often tempting to raid the costume store for anything that broadly fits the bill but the result is likely to be a hotchpotch of odd attire that just confuses the audience. The principle here should be to keep it as simple as possible, using costume to enhance and clarify rather than to decorate. Plain coloured tee-shirts will often do the job very well. So, for example, when performing your version of Agincourt in *Henry V* you might have all the English soldiers in red tee-shirts and all the French in blue. In *The Tempest*, you might have a rich magic cloak that Prospero wears which contrasts with everyone else's simple costume.

Sound and light

Here, too, a simple approach is likely to work best. If you are going to use stage lighting at all, it will probably be no more than a general wash. Other lighting effects can be done very simply. Imagine, for example, that the hall is blacked out for the opening scene of *Hamlet* that we described in Chapter 4 but that each of the children carries an electric torch. These can be used to search, to light each other's faces in the darkness or to swing round suddenly and light the ghost – very simple but highly effective. But do remember that much of the children's work may be best served by no more than natural daylight or the everyday lighting in your hall.

Those same principles of simplicity and playful invention also apply to how you might use sound. As we suggested in Chapter 4, recorded music can enhance something like the enacting of a battle. But a much simpler use of sound and music can add to a performance in all sorts of ways. When the ghost of Hamlet's father is speaking, for example, you might have performers adding sounds with percussion instruments every time murder or revenge is mentioned. These sounds can then become motifs that are repeated throughout the performance and come to a crescendo in the final scene. Remember, too, that children can make a wide range of sounds with their voices, their bodies and with everyday objects – just as they do when they create the storm from *The Tempest* in Chapter 2. Creating sound inventively and playfully can be just as effective in performance.

Involving everyone

In *Beginning Drama 4–11* (2008) we include a checklist for those running a production in a primary school. We stress the need to involve other staff as early as possible. Not only does this help to share the work, it also helps to build a sense that this is something in which the whole school has an investment, something *we* have created together. If you are creating work through the kinds of active approaches we have outlined, children are very likely to tell their parents all about it from the start. So it is worth keeping parents updated – verbally, through newsletters, or perhaps through a blog on the school website – so that a sense of excitement and anticipation grows as the performance date draws near.

Work to enhance the performance

At its best, this kind of ensemble performance can reach right across the primary curriculum. In doing this, you can draw inspiration from professional theatre practice. Your programme, for instance, might include much more than just a cast list. Children might write articles about the play, its story and its history. What really happened at the battle of Agincourt? What happened in a medieval siege like that at Harfleur? How has Henry V been portrayed on film? The programme might also include some photographs of the performance in rehearsal. A synopsis of the plot is often included as well and can be very helpful for members of the audience who do not know the play at all. Who will design the posters? What other means will you use to publicise the event? Who will manage all the front-of-house arrangements? Rather than see such questions as problems to be overcome, turn them into opportunities to make the project as rich as it can be and involve as many members of the school community as possible.

In the two examples that follow, we outline how two of the plays we explored earlier translate into the kind of performance that best reflects and celebrates all that the children have learned in their early encounters with Shakespeare.

Example 1 – *The Tempest*

This performance by six- and seven-year-olds takes place in the afternoon. They have worked on the play and its themes throughout the term. The school hall is packed with parents, grandparents and siblings who are seated on three sides, leaving a performance space in the middle. The children enter in silence, form a circle and sit. One child then stands, collects a cloak and a staff that have already been placed at the back of the space, puts the cloak on and walks to the centre of the circle. He lowers his staff so that it is touching the floor and then slowly raises it. The further he lifts it, the more the sound from the rest of the performers builds: starting with gentle finger tapping on the floor, building to clapping, then adding voices to suggest wind and rain, then feet start drumming on the floor to create the effect of thunder. As the staff is lowered, the sound dies down again, the child replaces the cloak and staff and returns to his place in the circle.

Now a group of children move into the circle and create a ship using themselves and a simple piece of cloth to represent the sail. The ship rocks gently at first, but then begins to move more violently. As it does so the sound from the rest of the circle builds again but this time with lines like 'A plague upon this howling!', 'We split! We split!' and 'Mercy on us!' added until it reaches a climax and the ship collapses into a shipwreck. Another child now goes and collects the staff and makes a 'whoosh' sound and action across the circle, just as her teacher has done throughout their work on the play. The children representing the ship return to their places.

The child holding the staff is one of a number who have been really excited by the story and have asked if they can borrow the story stick at playtime. The teacher notices that they are using it to tell the story of Prospero, Duke of Milan, and his daughter Miranda over and over, mimicking the way she told the story and even including what they remember of Shakespeare's language. She builds on this enthusiasm to develop their skills as storytellers and, between them, they are now taking responsibility for telling the story, passing the story stick from one to another as they do. One of them begins by holding the stick and saying, 'This shipwreck happened on an island far away. It was caused by a great magician called Prospero and he did it because of something that happened many years earlier in the city of Milan.' In just the way that they heard the story in the first place, the children now tell the story of Prospero, his daughter Miranda and his brother Antonio. The major difference from the original is that the children know who will enter the circle and when and have prepared their shared telling so that it is really clear to everyone watching. But it still retains all the energy and playful inventiveness of the original telling. Together the children tell the story up to the point where Prospero and Miranda land on their island.

In their music lessons, the children have taken these lines and turned them into a song:

> The isle is full of noises,
> Sounds, and sweet airs, that give delight and hurt not.
> Sometimes, a thousand twangling instruments
> Will hum about mine ears.

They sing the song together as they move around the stage as if exploring the island for the first time, looking over, under and around things, looking out into the audience with delight, excitement and fascination. Then one of the storytellers holds up the story stick and freezes the action. She narrates, 'But there was someone living on the island already and his name was Caliban – "a freckled whelp, hag-born, not honoured with a human shape"'. All the children pick up this line and repeat it together over and over. Each time they say the line they take up a new 'Caliban freeze' and look out into the audience contorting their faces and bodies in different ways. They do this ten times. After the last time they move into pairs. In these pairs they move around the island as Miranda and Caliban exploring together. A cymbal signals that they must freeze and all the Mirandas now chant 'Caliban, Caliban, what can you see?'. The Calibans take it in turn to reply using language from the play like 'I see brine pits, that's what I see'. When the game has been repeated enough times for all the Calibans to speak, the children return to their circle. One of the storytellers takes the staff and tells how Caliban woke one night and tried to kiss Miranda. The child playing Prospero awakes with the line 'Hag seed! Abhorrèd slave!' and the storyteller 'whooshes' the circle clear. With one child taking the staff from the storyteller, the others move to the edges of the stage and take up Caliban poses ready to play 'Caliban's footsteps'. The game is played much as it was in class but the children give even greater attention to how Caliban moves and shows his resentment of Prospero. The nearer they get to him the louder the line 'This island is mine!' becomes until they reach a climax and Prospero 'whooshes' them all back to the edges of the stage. Now another child comes forward as storyteller, takes the staff from Prospero and tells the story of Ariel. Another child as Prospero takes the cloak and stick and calls his Ariel(s) unto him. They gather and link arms to form a circle that represents Prospero's magic cauldron. Using a combination of the spells they have written in class they chant together and make the spell to conjure the storm. Prospero moves to the edge of the stage and mimes pouring his potion into the sea.

Now the children return to the circle and repeat the storm, the ship and shipwreck that they did at the beginning of their performance. As the ship collapses into a wreck, one of the storytellers explains that all Prospero's enemies are on board and now he has them in his power. What should he do – seek virtue or vengeance? At this all the children stand and turn to the audience and ask in unison: 'Virtue or vengeance?' and their performance ends. It has lasted less than 45 minutes but has shown their work and understanding to remarkable effect. And everyone has performed Shakespeare.

Example 2 – *Henry V*

This piece is devised and performed by a group of ten- and eleven-year-olds. They have chosen to perform in their school hall in the evening, but the reception area of the school has been transformed with displays of their written work, photographs of them in rehearsal, their ideas for costume design, and a model showing how a wall could be undermined during a siege of a city like Harfleur. Parents, friends and family have arrived early, looked at the displays, been served drinks and cakes by staff and children from other classes, and gone into the hall with a real sense of excitement and anticipation. They take their seats on three sides of the performance space. There is no set as such, just a huge map of southern England and northern France that the children have painted on cloth. It shows London, Southampton, Harfleur, Calais and Agincourt. When everyone is in their seats, the hall goes dark.

The children enter from each corner of the hall, each carrying a torch. They use these to make their way safely to their places at the back of the audience. When everyone is in place, they all turn their torches off. Each child has learned a line from the opening chorus 'O, for a muse of fire . . .'. As they speak their line, they switch on their torch and direct the beam towards the central performance area. When the speech is complete, the lights come up, the torches are turned off and left at the edges of the hall.

One child is learning the trumpet and plays a simple fanfare as the king and his court enter the stage. Based on their exploration of Act I, Scene 2 as described in Chapter 4, the children perform it. They include the entry of the French Ambassadors and the gift of tennis balls. As the Ambassadors leave, the other children stand, turn to the audience and say together, 'This was a merry message'. King Henry stands, they kneel, and he says 'We hope to make the sender blush at it'. The children move to the edge of the stage and sit.

In their drama work, the children devised a shared performance of 'Now all the youth of England are on fire' from the beginning of Act II. What they put on the stage is pretty much the same piece, but they have worked hard to polish it so that everyone knows exactly what to do and when.

A very brief piece of active storytelling tells of the English Ambassadors visiting the French court. It finishes with everyone moving to the back of the stage (upstage) and speaking a few of the lines from the Chorus at the beginning of Act III:

> Suppose th'ambassador from the French comes back,
> Tells Harry that the king doth offer him
> Katherine his daughter, and with her, to dowry,
> Some petty and unprofitable dukedoms.
> The offer likes not, and the nimble gunner
> With linstock now the devilish cannon touches
> And down goes all before them.

As these lines are spoken, a group of children come and form a wall by linking arms. Others enact the firing of the cannon and a breach opens up in the wall the children have created. Those who are not part of the wall charge at the breach three times but each time turn back and regroup upstage. Each charge is highly disciplined and accompanied by loud war cries and screams. After the third charge, the whole class performs its shared version of 'Once more unto the breach . . .' building so they make a complete battle tableau that faces out towards the audience. As the last line, 'Cry "God for Harry, England, and Saint George!"' is spoken in unison, an English flag rises up to form the centre of the tableau.

Throughout, the children use the active ensemble storytelling to link the whole-class performance pieces. As they do this they use the map to make it clear how Henry leaves Harfleur in the charge of his uncle, the Duke of Exeter, and takes the rest of the English army to Calais. They narrate and enact what a difficult march it would have been in a wet autumn with sickness spreading among the troops. They tell and enact how the French army catches up with the English at Agincourt, and how Henry walks among his army the night before the battle. The whole class works together to perform the lines beginning 'But if the cause be not good' as we described in Chapter 4 with powerful images of the horror of battle. The contrast with the flag-waving heroics of 'Once more unto the breach' is powerful, as is their shared performance of the St Crispin's day speech. Many of the images from 'But if the cause be not good' are repeated when the class enacts the battle itself – a polished and highly disciplined version of the work the children did in class.

The stage clears for the numbering of the dead. The children have prepared 10,000 pieces of blue paper; one for each French soldier that died. They did this by using a hole-punch on sheets of blue card and keeping the circles that were punched out. It took a while to do, but they enjoyed coming in at lunchtimes and rattling off a couple of hundred at a time. As the numbers of French dead are read out, the children move around the stage letting the tiny circles fall from their hands and flutter to the floor. It is a spectacular and moving way of depicting just how many men were lost.

The collective performance of the speech from Act V, Scene 2 'Should not in this best garden of the world ...' is another powerful reflection of the cost of war. The children narrate and enact the marriage of Henry and Katherine, the French King's daughter. Their performance finishes with everyone speaking Henry's lines:

> Then shall I swear to Kate, and you to me,
> And may our oaths well kept and prosp'rous be!

It is important to stress that we offer these examples to show how the practical activity of earlier chapters might translate into performance. Your performances will be different because your shared explorations will lead you to different conclusions. But it is worth noting that both pieces make use of the original text, edited to fit the group's purpose and intentions. Neither makes use of a ready-made edit or attempts to translate the plays into 'modern English' – between you, you and your class will find more than enough to shape a powerful and moving performance from the extraordinary texts we have all inherited.

Chapter 7

Shakespeare, ambition and achievement

Previous chapters have shown how children's earliest encounters with Shakespeare can be active, playful and enjoyable. All the practical examples we have offered have been developed with children who have approached the work with confidence, excitement and that genuine sense of shared exploration and discovery which we have emphasised throughout.

But when we introduce Shakespeare so early, the ways in which we approach the plays and the responses children have to them can lead to two related problems in how such work is perceived by others. First, there are those who will merely smile indulgently, clap their hands with delight and say, 'Isn't it wonderful that children so young are doing Shakespeare!'. Well yes, it is, and we articulated some of the reasons why it is in the introduction. But without some clearer sense of what it might mean to do Shakespeare *well* at this age we would have to accept that all approaches, however suspect, are of equal worth. Second, there are those who take what might be described as a more Gradgrindian approach to education: deeply suspicious of children enjoying anything at all and believing that only hard facts, hard work and a decent dose of worthy misery offer the true course to educational achievement. For such people, the sort of work we have outlined is an unnecessary distraction from a properly utilitarian primary curriculum that focuses only on the 'basics'. And, of course, their ultimate expression of disdain for such work as ours is that it 'lacks rigour'. If we only recognise and appreciate children's work by smiling and clapping, the door is wide open to such criticism.

So what we outline in this chapter is a way of recognising and articulating clearly what children can achieve at various stages of their primary education. What we offer is certainly not intended as a set of attainment goals or targets: teachers the world over already have more than enough of those to keep them busy. As you read through the book, the more dutiful among you may feel an uncontrollable urge to turn it all into grids and checklists but we would ask you to resist such a temptation at all costs. What we show here is what we know children *can* achieve at various stages: we know because we have seen it happen. Once we let that become what children *should* achieve, the grids and checklists become ends in themselves and are in danger of suffocating the very work that gave rise to them. Such grids and lists also tend to focus on individual contributions at the expense of what has been achieved by the whole class working as an ensemble. Of course, we would encourage you to celebrate what you and your class can do together; but you should do so in the knowledge that you do it all through choice rather than prescription.

We organise our suggestions under three closely related headings: engaging with Shakespeare's plays and their stories; exploring text; and performing. We suggest what is achievable by many, even most, children at the ages of seven, nine and eleven. In doing so it is important to stress that this is not about 'more able' children or those who have been designated elsewhere as 'gifted and talented'. Our experience of working with a great many teachers and their classes has shown that they are very often surprised and delighted by who takes to this work and engages with it most. All the best teachers have clear and high expectations of the children they teach but they are also more than willing to be surprised and to see those expectations exceeded.

Expectations at the age of seven

Engaging with Shakespeare's plays and their stories

Between the ages of four and seven children may have encountered one or two of the plays. They will be able to name them, tell you who some of the characters are and tell you something of the plot. When you tell the stories together, they will engage actively, be eager to re-tell the story so far and speculate about what might happen next. They will tell you who their favourite characters are and why, and comment on characters' actions, intentions and feelings. They will work together playfully to imagine and create the worlds of the plays through language, objects and action.

Exploring text

At this stage, most children will encounter Shakespeare's language by hearing and repeating it. This will be done playfully through games and through joining in when you tell and enact the stories together. They will respond to the patterns and rhythms of Shakespeare's language in the same way as they do to rhyme and song, associating them with action. In response to a question like 'Who can tell us some lines from a Shakespeare play?' they can readily offer two or three examples, probably adding actions as they do so. They may begin to use some of Shakespeare's language in their talk and writing.

Performing

Children will work together and collaborate with their teacher to create performances that are playfully, yet clearly, telling a story. They will make suggestions for how the story, its characters and its setting can be made clear for an audience. They will join in telling the story, knowing when and how their contribution is needed. When they speak the language, they will do so clearly and confidently.

They will approach their performances with assurance, pride and delight and will be eager to share their work with as many people as possible.

Expectations at the age of nine

Engaging with Shakespeare's plays and their stories

By the age of nine children may have explored three or four of the plays. They will be able to name them, provide some plot details and identify the kind of stories that they tell, perhaps distinguishing between comedies and tragedies. They will work in groups to bring parts of the story to life through images and language and contribute these to a whole class telling. As they do so, they will speculate about the story: its themes, its characters and their actions, motives and feelings. They will work together to create and bring to life the settings of the plays, understanding that there are many ways in which they can be interpreted. They will begin to support their ideas by reference to the text.

Exploring text

At this stage children will read Shakespeare's text as a whole class and in groups. They will perform the language on their feet, adding it to short scenes and images that they have created together. They will begin to understand how the text is open to interpretation and can be spoken in many ways and they will enjoy doing this in pairs and groups. Through repeating and playing with the language, they will become more aware of its patterns and rhythms. They will begin to use some of Shakespeare's language in their talk and writing.

Performing

Children will work in groups and as a whole class, collaborating with their teacher to create performances that are inventively and clearly telling a story. They will make suggestions for how the story – its plot, characters and settings – can be made clear for an audience. They will work together, knowing when and how their different contributions are needed. When they speak the language, they will do so clearly, confidently and with meaning. They will experiment with ideas for how props, costumes, sound and light can enhance their work. They will approach their performances with assurance, pride and delight and will be eager to share their work with as many people as possible.

Expectations at the age of eleven

Engaging with Shakespeare's plays and their stories

By the age of eleven children may have explored five or six of the plays. They will be able to name them, give an outline of their plots and identify the kind of stories that they tell, distinguishing between comedies, histories and tragedies. They will work in pairs and groups to bring parts of the story to life through images and language and contribute these to the whole class's growing understanding of the play. As they do so, they will speculate about the story: its themes, its characters and their actions, motives and feelings. They will back their ideas up with discoveries made through exploring the text together. They will use evidence from the text to create and bring to life the settings of the plays, understanding that there are many ways in which they can be interpreted. Although the teacher will continue to offer an overview of the plot and add narrative links between scenes and text extracts that they explore together, children's understanding of the stories will also be informed by working directly from the text. They will begin to make connections between the different plays they have explored.

Exploring text

At this stage children will read Shakespeare's text as a whole class, in groups, in pairs and individually, sharing what they discover and learn as they go. They will perform the language on their feet, experimenting with different possibilities and interpretations. They will understand how the text is open to interpretation and can be spoken in many ways and they will enjoy doing this in pairs and in groups, offering their work for discussion with the rest of the class. Through repeatedly experimenting with the language, they will enjoy discovering its patterns and rhythms and will begin to relate this to how Shakespeare's characters might feel and act. They will include some of Shakespeare's language in their talk and writing and will use what they have learned to create rhythmic and patterned writing of their own.

Performing

Children will work in groups and as a whole class, collaborating with their teacher to create performances that are clear, inventive and coherent. They will experiment together before making choices for how the story – its plot, characters and settings – can best be made clear for an audience. They will work together to tell the story, knowing when and how their different contributions are needed and understanding how they work as an ensemble. When they speak the language, they will do so clearly, confidently and meaningfully, using what they have learned as they explored the text together. They will use props, costumes, sound and light creatively, coherently and thoughtfully to enhance their performances. They will approach their performances with assurance, pride and delight, eager to share their work with as many people as possible. They will enjoy working with younger children to advise, support and guide them in developing performances of their own.

We should stress that these expectations are deliberately ambitious and cannot be realised easily or quickly. To begin to meet them will require a whole-school commitment to embedding Shakespeare throughout the primary age range. A teacher of eleven-year-olds who is new to teaching Shakespeare would, quite understandably, look at our expectations for that age with more than a little incredulity – as if she doesn't have enough to do already! But if she chose, for example, to try some of the ideas for exploring *Henry V* that we outlined in Chapter 4, that in itself should be more than enough cause for recognition and celebration. In doing so she may have set in train a process that will lead to other teachers asking about what she did and how, wondering if she has any ideas for how they might introduce some of the plays with their own classes. Once they make a start and the children get excited about the plays, the whole school could be off and running. But we suggest that it is only *after* that process has been going on for some time that you begin to refer to and share the expectations we have outlined here. Then, and only then, might you use them to celebrate what you have achieved together, rather than to induce any sense of inadequacy or failure because of what you have yet to do. Trust in the kind of active approaches we have outlined and you may be surprised by just how far you all get. And, as we emphasised earlier, we offer them primarily so that you can recognise your achievements and shout them from the rooftops. Even if you try just one or two of the active approaches in this book, you may have given that group of children a much richer and more enjoyable introduction to Shakespeare than they would have had otherwise. That alone is more than enough cause for celebration.

The story of Prospero's lost dukedom

This story is based on Act I, Scene 2 of *The Tempest*. It is intended to be used as part of the work on the play that we include in Chapter 3. Chapter 2 outlines the 'story stick' or 'story wand' technique, which would probably be the most effective way of telling it with your class. As you do this, you could read this version of the story aloud or you might choose to learn it so that you can watch the children carefully and incorporate their ideas as you go along. There is more guidance on how to do this in Chapter 2 of *Beginning Drama 4–11* (2008). Text in quotes is taken directly from the play and can be used to create the 'text scraps' that we refer to in Chapter 3.

Once upon a time in a city called Milan there lived a Duke called Prospero. 'He was Duke of Milan and a prince of power.' Prospero was a good duke and his people loved him. As he walked the streets of Milan the people would clap and cheer and he would wave back. Everyone was very happy.

Although he loved his people greatly, there were two other loves in Prospero's life. The first was his daughter, Miranda. Miranda 'wast not out three years old' and her father was most devoted to her. But his other great love was his library: books, books and more books, 'volumes he prized above his dukedom'. And do you know what he studied in those books? The art of magic! Prospero was 'rapt in secret studies' that would make him a very great magician.

Now Prospero had a brother named Antonio. Prospero loved his brother and trusted him completely. So one day he called everyone together and announced 'The government I cast upon my brother'. He would let his brother Antonio do the work of the duke in his place. And Prospero taught his brother how to be a good duke: 'how to grant suits, how to deny them, who t'advance and who to trash for over-topping'.

But in Prospero's 'false brother awakened an evil nature'. Why, he thought to himself, should I do the work of a duke and not be a duke? Antonio, Prospero's 'false brother' and Miranda's 'false uncle', got on his horse and rode to the city of Naples.

Now, the King of Naples was called Alonso and he was an 'enemy inveterate' of Duke Prospero. How terrible then that Antonio should hatch a plot with Alonso to overthrow Prospero – but that is just what he did! They agreed that Alonso would send a 'treacherous army' to help Antonio take over the city of Milan.

The soldiers crept up on Prospero and Miranda in the dead of night. They tied them up and led them to the gates of the city. 'Fated to th'purpose, did Antonio open the gates of Milan, and i'th'dead of darkness' led the duke and his daughter to a ship that would take them away from the city forever!

Now there was a good servant whose name was Gonzalo. Though there was little he could do to stop the soldiers, he gave Prospero and his daughter food and fresh water to take on their journey. And he gave them 'rich garments, linens, stuffs and necessaries'. Most important of all, he gave Prospero books from his library – 'volumes he prized above his dukedom'.

But once the ship had borne them some 'leagues to sea', Antonio's villains had prepared 'a rotten carcass of a butt, not rigged, nor tackle, sail, nor mast: the very rats instinctively have quit it'. Without a care for their safety, Prospero and Miranda were set adrift in this rotten old boat, a boat that the waves might swallow at any moment ...

The sea roared and the winds sighed and the little boat was tossed about on the waves. Prospero feared greatly for their lives, and it was only Miranda's trusting smile, 'infusèd with a fortitude from heaven', that kept him alive.

But, by and by, the winds calmed. As Prospero looked out from this 'rotten carcass of a butt', he could see an island in the distance. It was beautiful and the closer they got, the more they could hear its beautiful 'sounds and sweet airs'. 'By providence divine', their little boat drifted towards the island and they landed safely on its shore.

Notes

Introduction

1 See 'Stand Up For Shakespeare' (2008) www.rsc.org.uk/education/sufs/
2 See Berry (2008) p. 14.

1 Beginning Shakespeare with games

1 See Cook (2000) p. 128.

2 Beginning Shakespeare with his stories

1 A detailed description of how to do this well is provided in *Beginning Drama 4–11*, pp. 28–31.
2 These issues are raised at different points in the story. See Winston (2000) for ways of incorporating their consideration into your planning and teaching.

Suggestions for further reading

Bate, J. (1998) *The Genius of Shakespeare*, London: Picador.

Berry, C. (2008) *From Word to Play*, London: Oberon Books.

Cook, G. (2000) *Language Play, Language Learning*, Oxford: Oxford University Press.

Garfield, L. (1985) *Shakespeare Stories*, London: Gollancz.

Gibson, R. (1998) *Teaching Shakespeare: A Handbook for Teachers*, Cambridge University Press.

Gibson, R. (2000) *Stepping into Shakespeare: Practical ways of Teaching Shakespeare*, Cambridge University Press.

Greenblatt, S. (2005) *Will in the World: How Shakespeare Became Shakespeare*, London: Pimlico.

Neelands, J. and Goode, T. (2000) *Structuring Drama Work*, Cambridge University Press.

Rosen, M. and Ingpen, R. (2001) *Shakespeare: His Work and His World*, London: Walker Books.

Royal Shakespeare Company (2010) *The RSC Shakespeare Toolkit for Teachers*, London: Methuen Drama.

Shapiro, J. (2006) *1599: A Year in the Life of William Shakespeare*, London: Faber & Faber.

Stredder, J. (2009) *The North Face of Shakespeare: Activities for Teaching the Plays*, Cambridge School Shakespeare, Cambridge University Press.

Tandy, M. and Howell, J. (2009) *Creating Drama with 4–7 Year Olds*, London: David Fulton.

Tandy, M. and Howell, J. (2009) *Creating Drama with 7–11 Year Olds*, London: David Fulton.

Winston, J. and Tandy, M. (2008) *Beginning Drama 4–11* (3rd edition), London: David Fulton.

Winston, J. (2000) *Drama, Literacy and Moral Education 5–11*, London: David Fulton.

Winston, J. (2004) *Drama and English at the Heart of the Curriculum*, London: David Fulton.

Winston, J. (2010) *Beauty and Education*, New York: Routledge.

Winston, J. (2012) "'Play is the Things'. Shakespeare, Language Play and Pedagogy in the Early Years", in *Journal of Aesthetic Education*, vol. 46, no. 3.

Index